Ian Maclaren

Afterwards

And other stories

Ian Maclaren

Afterwards
And other stories

ISBN/EAN: 9783741181566

Manufactured in Europe, USA, Canada, Australia, Japa

Cover: Foto ©Andreas Hilbeck / pixelio.de

Manufactured and distributed by brebook publishing software (www.brebook.com)

Ian Maclaren

Afterwards

WORKS BY IAN MACLAREN

Beside the Bonnie Brier Bush
The Days of Auld Lang Syne
A Doctor of the Old School
Kate Carnegie
Afterwards
The Upper Room
The Mind of The Master
The Cure of Souls
The Potter's Wheel
Companions of the Sorrowful Way
The Ian Maclaren Year-Book

AFTERWARDS

AND OTHER STORIES

BY

IAN MACLAREN

NEW YORK
DODD, MEAD & COMPANY
1898

COPYRIGHT, 1895, 1896, BY THE S. S. MCCLURE COMPANY.

COPYRIGHT, 1895, 1896, 1897, 1898, BY JOHN WATSON.

COPYRIGHT, 1898, BY DODD, MEAD & COMPANY.

BURR PRINTING HOUSE, NEW YORK.

CONTENTS

CHAPTER		PAGE
I.	Afterwards	3
II.	The Minister of St. Bede's	37
III.	An Impossible Man	73
IV.	Righteous Over Much	93
V.	A Probationer	115
VI.	A Government Official	137
VII.	The Right Hand of Samuel Dodson	157
VIII.	Saved by Faith	201
IX.	The Last Sacrifice	225
X.	An Evangelist	245
XI.	The Collector's Inconsistency	269
XII.	Father Jinks	301
XIII.	The Passing of Domsie	339
XIV.	Dr. Davidson's Last Christmas	359

AFTERWARDS

AFTERWARDS

AND OTHER STORIES

AFTERWARDS

I

He received the telegram in a garden, where he was gazing on a vision of blue, set in the fronds of a palm, and listening to the song of the fishers, as it floated across the bay.

"You look so utterly satisfied," said his hostess, in the high, clear voice of Englishwomen, "that I know you are tasting the luxury of a contrast. The Riviera is charming in December; imagine London, and Cannes is Paradise."

As he smiled assent in the grateful laziness of a hard-worked man, his mind was stung with the remembrance of a young wife swathed in the dreary fog, who, above all things, loved the open air and the shining of the sun.

Her plea was that Bertie would weary alone, and that she hated travelling, but it came to him quite suddenly that this was always the programme of their holidays—some Mediterranean villa, full of clever people, for him, and the awful dulness of that Bloomsbury street for her; or he went North to a shooting-lodge, where he told his best stories in the smoking-room, after a long day on the purple heather; and she did her best for Bertie at some watering-place, much frequented on account of its railway facilities and economical lodgings. Letters of invitation had generally a polite reference to his wife—"If Mrs. Trevor can accompany you I shall be still more delighted"—but it was understood that she would not accept.

"We have quite a grudge against Mrs. Trevor, because she will never come with her husband; there is some beautiful child who monopolises her," his hostess would explain on his arrival; and Trevor allowed it to be understood that his wife was quite devoted to Bertie, and would be miserable without him.

When he left the room, it was explained: "Mrs. Trevor is a hopelessly quiet person, what is called a 'good wife,' you know."

"The only time she dined with us, Tottie Fribbyl —he was a Theosophist then, it's two years ago—was too amusing for words, and told us what incarnation he was going through.

"Mrs. Trevor, I believe, had never heard of Theosophy, and looked quite horrified at the idea of poor Tottie's incarnation.

"'Isn't it profane to use such words?' she said

to me. So I changed to skirt dancing, and would you believe me, she had never seen it?

"What can you do with a woman like that? Nothing remains but religion and the nursery. Why do clever men marry those impossible women?"

Trevor was gradually given to understand, as by an atmosphere, that he was a brilliant man wedded to a dull wife, and there were hours—his worst hours—when he agreed.

Cara mia, cara mia, sang the sailors; and his wife's face in its perfect refinement and sweet beauty suddenly replaced the Mediterranean.

Had he belittled his wife, with her wealth of sacrifice and delicate nature, beside women in spectacles who wrote on the bondage of marriage, and leaders of fashion who could talk of everything from horse-racing to palmistry?

He had only glanced at her last letter; now he read it carefully:—

"The flowers were lovely, and it was so mindful of you to send them, just like my husband. Bertie and I amused ourselves arranging and rearranging them in glasses, till we had made our tea-table lovely. But I was just one little bit disappointed not to get a letter—you see how exacting I am, sir. I waited for every post, and Bertie said, 'Has father's letter come yet?' When one is on holiday, writing letters is an awful bore; but please just a line to Bertie and me. We have a map of the Riviera, and found out all the places you have visited in the yacht; and we tried to imagine you sailing on that azure sea, and landing among those silver olives. I am so grateful to every one for being kind to you, and I hope you will enjoy yourself to the full. Bertie is a little stronger, I'm sure; his cheeks were quite rosy to-day for him. It was his birthday on Wednesday, and I gave him a little treat. The sun was shining brightly in the forenoon, and we had a walk in the Gardens, and made believe that it was Italy! Then we went to Oxford Street, and Bertie chose a regiment of soldiers for his birthday present. He wished some guns so much that I allowed him to have them as a present from you. They only cost one-and-sixpence, and I thought you would like him to have something. Jane and he had a splendid game of hide-and-seek in the evening, and my couch was the den, so you see we have our own gaiety in Bloomsbury.

"Don't look sulky at this long scribble and say, 'What nonsense women write!' for it is almost the same as speaking to you, and I shall imagine the letter all the way till you open it in the sunshine.

"So smile and kiss my name, for this comes with my heart's love from
    "Your devoted wife,
      "MAUD TREVOR.

"P.S.—Don't be alarmed because I have to rest;

the doctor does not think that there is any danger, and I'll take great care."

"A telegram." It was the shattering of a dream. "How wicked of some horrid person. Business ought not to be allowed to enter Paradise. Let's hope it's pleasure; perhaps some one has won a lot of money at Monte Carlo, and wishes us to celebrate the affair.

"Whom is it for? Oh! Mr. Edward Trevor; then it's a brief by telegraph, I suppose. Some millionaire's will case, and the Attorney-General can't manage it alone. What a man he is, to have briefs in holiday time.

"There it is, but remember, before you open it, that you are bound to remain here over Christmas at any rate, and help us with our theatricals. My husband declares that a successful barrister must be a born actor." . . .

An hour later Trevor was in the Paris express, and for thirty hours he prayed one petition, that she might live till he arrived. He used to have a berth in the Wagon Lit as a matter of course, and had begun to complain about the champagne in the dining-car, but the thought of comfort made him wince on this journey, and he twice changed his carriage, once when an English party would not cease from badinage that mocked his ears, and again because a woman had brown eyes with her expression of dog-like faithfulness. The darkness of the night after that sunlit garden, and the monotonous roar of the train, and the face of smiling France covered with snow, and the yeasty waters of the Channel, and the moaning of the wind, filled his heart with dread.

Will that procession of luggage at Dover never come to an end? A French seaman—a fellow with earrings and a merry face—appears and reappears with maddening regularity, each time with a larger trunk. One had X. Y. on it in big white letters. Why not Z. also? Who could have such a name? That is a lady's box, black and brown, plastered with hotel labels. Some bride, perhaps . . . They are carrying the luggage over his heart. Have they no mercy?

The last piece is in, and the sailors make a merry group at the top of the gangway. They look like Bretons, and that fellow is laughing again —some story about a little child; he can just hear *Ma petite*. . . .

"Guard, is this train never to start? We're half-an-hour late already."

"Italian mail very heavy, sir; still bringing up bags; so many people at Riviera in winter, writing home to their friends." . . .

How cruel every one is! He had not written for ten days. Something always happened, an engagement of pleasure. There was a half-finished letter; he had left it to join a Monte Carlo party.

"Writing letters—home, of course, to that idolised wife. It's beautiful, and you are an example to us all; but Mrs. Trevor will excuse descriptions of scenery; she knows you are enjoying yourself."

Had she been expecting that letter from post to post, calculating the hour of each delivery, identifying the postman's feet in that quiet street, holding her breath when he rang, stretching her hand for a letter, to let it drop unopened, and bury her face in the pillow? Had she died waiting for a letter that never came? Those letters that he wrote from the Northern Circuit in that first sweet year, a letter a day, and one day two—it had given him a day's advantage over her. Careful letters, too, though written between cases, with bits of description and amusing scenes. Some little sameness towards the end, but she never complained of that, and even said those words were the best. And that trick he played—the thought of the postman must have brought it up—how pleasant it was, and what a success! He would be his own letter one day, and take her by surprise. "A letter, ma'am," the girl said—quite a homely girl, who shared their little joys and anxieties—and then he showed his face with apologies for intrusion. The flush of love in her face, will it be like that to-night, or . . . What can be keeping the train now? Is this a conspiracy to torment a miserable man?

He thrusts his head out of the window in despair, and sees the guard trying to find a compartment for a family that had mistaken their train.

The husband is explaining, with English garrulity, all the station hearing, what an inconvenience it would have been had they gone in the Holborn Viaduct carriages.

"Half an hour's longer drive, you know, and it's very important we should get home in time; we are expected . . ."

For what? Dinner, most likely. What did it matter when they got home, to-day or next year? Yet he used to be angry if he were made late for dinner. They come into his compartment, and explain the situation at great length, while he pretends to listen.

A husband and wife returning from a month in Italy, full of their experiences: the Corniche Road, the palaces of Genoa, the pictures in the Pitti, St. Peter's at Rome. Her first visit to the Continent, evidently; it reminded them of a certain tour round the Lakes in '80, and she withdrew her hand from her husband's as the train came out from the tunnel. They were not smart people—very pronounced middle-class—but they were lovers, after fifteen years.

They forgot him, who was staring on the bleak landscape with white, pinched face.

"How kind to take me this trip. I know how much you denied yourself, but it has made me young again," and she said "Edward." Were all these coincidences arranged? had his purgatorio begun already?

"Have you seen the *Globe*, sir? Bosworth, M.P. for Pedlington, has been made a judge, and there's to be a keen contest.

"Trevor, I see, is named as the Tory candidate—a clever fellow, I've heard. Do you know about him? he's got on quicker than any man of his years.

"Some say that it's his manner; he's such a good sort, the juries cannot resist him, a man told me—a kind heart goes for something even in a lawyer. Would you like to look? . . .

"Very sorry; would you take a drop of brandy? No? The passage was a little rough, and you don't look quite up to the mark."

Then they left him in peace, and he drank his cup to the dregs.

It was for Pedlington he had been working and saving, for a seat meant society and the bench, perhaps. . . . What did it matter now?

She was to come and sit within the cage when he made his first speech, and hear all the remarks.

"Of course it will be a success, for you do everything well, and your wife will be the proudest woman in London.

"Sir Edward Trevor, M.P. I know it's foolish, but it's the foolishness of love, dear, so don't look cross; you are everything to me, and no one loves you as I do."

What are they slowing for now? There's no station. Did ever train drag like this one?

Off again, thank God . . . if she only were

conscious, and he could ask her to forgive his selfishness.

At last, and the train glides into Victoria. No, he had nothing to declare; would they let him go, or they might keep his luggage altogether.

Some vision was ever coming up, and now he saw her kneeling on the floor and packing that portmanteau, the droop of her figure, her thin white hands.

He was so busy that she did these offices for him—tried to buckle the straps even; but he insisted on doing that. It gave him half an hour longer at the Club. What a brute he had been. . . .

"Do anything you like with my things. I'll come to-morrow . . . as fast as you can drive."

Huddled in a corner of the hansom so that you might have thought he slept, this man was calculating every foot of the way, gloating over a long stretch of open, glistening asphalt, hating unto murder the immovable drivers whose huge vans blocked his passage. If they had known, there was no living man but would have made room for him . . . but he had not known himself. . . . Only one word to tell her he knew now.

As the hansom turned into the street he bent forward, straining his eyes to catch the first glimpse of home. Had it been day-time the blinds would have told their tale; now it was the light he watched.

Dark on the upper floors; no sick light burn-

AFTERWARDS

ing . . . have mercy . . . then the blood came back to his heart with a rush. How could he have forgotten?

Their room was at the back for quietness, and it might still be well. Some one had been watching, for the door was instantly opened, but he could not see the servant's face.

A doctor came forward and beckoned him to go into the study. . . .

It seemed as if his whole nature had been smitten with insensibility, for he knew everything without words, and yet he heard the driver demanding his fare, and noticed that the doctor had been reading the evening paper while he waited; he saw the paragraph about that seat.

What work those doctors have to do. . . .

"It was an hour ago . . . we were amazed that she lived so long; with any other woman it would have been this morning; but she was determined to live till you came home.

"It was not exactly will-power, for she was the gentlest patient I ever had; it was"—the doctor hesitated—a peremptory Scotchman hiding a heart of fire beneath a coating of ice—"it was simply love."

When the doctor had folded up the evening paper, and laid it on a side table, which took some time, he sat down opposite that fixed, haggard face, which had not yet been softened by a tear.

"Yes, I'll tell you everything if you desire me;

perhaps it will relieve your mind; and Mrs. Trevor said you would wish to know, and I must be here to receive you. Her patience and thoughtfulness were marvellous.

"I attend many very clever and charming women, but I tell you, Mr. Trevor, not one has so impressed me as your wife. Her self-forgetfulness passed words; she thought of every one except herself; why, one of the last things she did was to give directions about your room; she was afraid you might feel the change from the Riviera. But that is by the way, and these things are not my business.

"From the beginning I was alarmed, and urged that you should be sent for; but she pledged me not to write; you needed your holiday, she said, and it must not be darkened with anxiety.

"She spoke every day about your devotion and unselfishness; how you wished her to go with you, but she had to stay with the boy. . . .

"The turn for the worse? it was yesterday morning, and I had Sir Reginald at once. We agreed that recovery was hopeless, and I telegraphed to you without delay.

"We also consulted whether she ought to be told, and Sir Reginald said, 'Certainly; that woman has no fear, for she never thinks of herself, and she will want to leave messages.'

"'If we can only keep her alive till to-morrow afternoon,' he said, and you will like to remember that everything known to the best man in London was done. Sir Reginald came back himself unasked to-day, because he remembered a restorative that might sustain the failing strength. She thanked him so sweetly that he was quite shaken; the fact is, that both of us would soon have played the fool. But I ought not to trouble you with these trifles at this time, only as you wanted to know all. . . .

"Yes, she understood what we thought before I spoke, and only asked when you would arrive. 'I want to say "Good-bye," and then I will be ready,' but perhaps. . . .

"'Tell you everything?' That is what I am trying to do, and I was here nearly all day, for I had hoped we might manage to fulfil her wish.

"No, she did not speak much, for we enjoyed silence and rest as the only chance; but she had your photograph on the pillow, and some flowers you had sent.

"They were withered, and the nurse removed them when she was sleeping; but she missed them, and we had to put them in her hands. 'My husband was so thoughtful.'

"This is too much for you, I see; it is simply torture. Wait till to-morrow. . . .

"Well, if you insist. Expecting a letter . . . yes . . . let me recollect. . . . No, I am not hiding anything, but you must not let this get upon your mind.

"We would have deceived her, but she knew the

hour of the Continental mails, and could detect the postman's ring. Once a letter came, and she insisted upon seeing it in case of any mistake. But it was only an invitation for you, I think, to some country house.

"It can't be helped now, and you ought not to vex yourself; but I believe a letter would have done more for her than . . . What am I saying now?

"As she grew weaker she counted the hours, and I left her at four full of hope. 'Two hours more and he'll be here,' and by that time she had your telegram in her hand.

"When I came back the change had come, and she said, 'It's not God's will; bring Bertie.'

"So she kissed him, and said something to him, but we did not listen. After the nurse had carried him out—for he was weeping bitterly, poor little chap—she whispered to me to get a sheet of paper and sit down by her bedside. . . . I think it would be better . . . very well, I will tell you all.

"I wrote what she dictated with her last breath, and I promised you would receive it from her own hand, and so you will. She turned her face to the door and lay quite still till about six, when I heard her say your name very softly, and a minute afterwards she was gone, without pain or struggle." . . .

She lay as she had died, waiting for his coming,

and the smile with which she had said his name was still on her face. It was the first time she did not colour with joy at his coming, that her hand was cold to his touch. He kissed her, but his heart was numbed, and he could not weep.

Then he took her letter and read it beside that silence.

"Dearest,—

They tell me now that I shall not live to see you come in and to cast my arms once more round your neck before we part. Be kind to Bertie, and remember that he is delicate and shy. He will miss me, and you will be patient with him for my sake. Give him my watch, and do not let him forget me. My locket with your likeness I would like left on my heart. You will never know how much I have loved you, for I could never speak. You have been very good to me, and I want you to know that I am grateful; but it is better perhaps that I should die, for I might hinder you in your future life. Forgive me because I came short of what your wife should have been. None can ever love you better. You will take these poor words from a dead hand, but I shall see you, and I shall never cease to love you, to follow your life, to pray for you—my first, my only love."

The fountains within him were broken, and he flung himself down by the bedside in an agony of repentance.

"Oh, if I had known before; but now it is too late, too late!"

For we sin against our dearest not because we do not love, but because we do not imagine.

II

Maud Trevor was a genuine woman, and kept her accounts with the aid of six purses. One was an ancient housewife of her grandmother's, which used to be equipped with silk and thread and needles and buttons, and from a secret place yielded to the third generation a bank note of value. This capacious receptacle was evidently intended for the household exchequer, whose transactions were innumerable, and whose monthly budget depended for success on an unfailing supply of copper. Another had come from her mother, and was of obsolete design—a bag closed at both extremities, with a long narrow slit in the middle, and two rings which compressed the gold into one end and the silver into the other. This was marked out by Providence for charity, since it made no provision for pennies, and laid a handicap of inconvenience on threepenny bits. It retained a subtle trace of an old-fashioned scent her mother loved, and recalled her mother going out on some errand of mercy—a St. Clare in her sacrifices and devotion. Purse three descended from her father, and was an incarnation of business—made of chamois leather with a steel clasp that closed with a click, having three compartments within, one of which had its own clasp and was reserved for gold. In this bank Maud kept the funds of a clothing society, whose more masterly bargains ran sometimes into farthings, and she was always haunted with anxiety lest a new farthing and a half sovereign should some day change places. A pretty little purse with ivory sides and silver hinges—a birthday gift of her girlhood—was large enough to hold her dress allowance, which Trevor had fixed at a most generous rate when he had barely four hundred a year, and had since forgotten to increase. One in sealskin had been a gift of engagement days, and held the savings of the year against birthday and Christmas presents—whose contents were the subject of many calculations. A cast-off purse of Trevor's had been devoted to Bertie, and from its resources came one way or other all he needed; but it happened that number six was constantly reinforced from the purse with the ivory sides.

Saturday afternoon was sacred to book-keeping, and Maud used her bed as a table for this critical operation, partly because it was so much larger than an escritoire, but chiefly because you could empty the purses into little pools with steep protecting banks. Of course if one sat down hurriedly there was great danger of amalgamation, with quite hopeless consequences; and Trevor held over Maud's head the chance of his making this mistake. It was his way, before he grew too busy, to watch till the anxious face would suddenly brighten and a rapid change be made in the pools—the household contributing something to presents and the dress purse to Bertie, while private and public charity would accommodate each other with change. Caresses were strictly forbidden in those times of abstruse calculation, and the Evil One who stands at every man's elbow once tempted Trevor to roll the counterpane into a bundle—purses, money, and all—but Maud, when he confessed, said that no human being would be allowed to fall into such wickedness.

Trevor was obliged to open her wardrobe, fourteen days after the funeral, and the first thing he lighted upon was the purses. They lay in a row on an old account-book—a motley set indeed—but so absurd and tricky a spirit is pathos, they affected him more swiftly than the sight of a portrait. Was ever any one so faithful and conscientious, so self-forgetful and kind, so capable also and clever in her own sphere? Latterly he had sneered at the purses, and once, being vexed at something in a letter, he had told Maud she ought to have done with that folly and keep her accounts like an educated woman. "A girl of twelve would be ashamed." . . . What a merciless power memory wields. She only drooped her head, . . . it was on the sealskin purse the tear fell, and at once he saw the bend of the Wye at Tintern where he had surprised her with the gift of that purse. He was moved to kiss away that tear, but his heart hardened. Why could she not be like the women he knew? . . . Well, he would not be troubled any longer with her simple ways . . . he could do as he pleased now with the purses. . . . A bitter madness of grief took possession of him, and he arranged them on the bed.

One was empty, the present purse, and he understood . . . the dress purse, of course, a little silver only . . . the rest had gone that he might have something beautiful. . . . He knew that it must be done sooner or later, and to-day was best, for his heart could be no sorer. . . . Yes, here they were, the ungiven gifts. For every person, from himself to the nurse; all wrapped in soft, white paper and ready in good time. . . . She used to arrange everything on Christmas Eve . . . this year he had intended to stay at Cannes, . . . there would just have been Bertie and his mother, now. . . . But he must open it—an inkstand for his study in solid brass, with pens and other things complete—he noted every detail as if to estimate its value. It came back to him how she had cunningly questioned him about his needs before he left for Cannes, till he grew impatient. "Don't bother me about ink-bottles." Yes, the very words, and others . . . the secret writing of memory came out in this fire of sorrow. "Why won't women understand that a man can't answer questions about trifles when he has work on hand?" He could swear to the words, and he knew how Maud looked, although he did not see.

"Don't go away; you promised that you would sit beside me when I worked—hinder me? I suppose you are bidding for a kiss; you know the sight of your face inspires me." . . . That was ten years ago . . . he might have borne with her presence a little longer. . . . She never would come again . . . he would have no interruptions of that kind. . . .

Her gloves, sixes—what a perfect hand it was (smoothes out the glove). His memory brings up a dinner table. Mrs. Chatterby gives her opinion on Meredith's last novel, and helps herself to salt —he sees a disgusting hand, with stumpy fingers, and, for impudence, a street arab of a thumb. A vulgar little woman through and through, and yet because she picked up scraps from the monthlies, and had the trick of catch-words, people paid her court. And he had sometimes thought, but he knew better to-day . . . of all things in the world a glove is the surest symbol. Mended, too, very neatly . . . that he might have his hansoms.

It was the last thing he ever could have imagined, and yet it must be a diary—Maud's diary! Turns over the leaves, and catches that woman's name against whom he has suddenly taken a violent dislike.

"January 25. Was at Mrs. Chatterby's—how strange one does not say anything of her husband —yet he is the nicer of the two—and I think it will be better not to go again to dinner. One can always make some excuse that will not be quite untrue.

"'The dinner is in honour of Mr. Fynical, who is leaving his College and coming to live in London, to do literary work,' as Mrs. Chatterby has been explaining for weeks, 'and to give tone to the weeklies.'

"'The younger men are quite devoted to him, and we ought all to be so thankful that he is to be within reach. His touch reminds one of,'—I don't know the French writer, but she does not always give the same name. 'We hope to see a great deal of him. So delightfully cynical, you know, and hates the bourgeoisie.'

"I was terrified lest I should sit next Mr. Fynical, but Mrs. Chatterby was merciful, and gave me Janie Godfrey's father. Edward says that he is a very able man, and will be Lord Chancellor some day, but he is so quiet and modest, that one feels quite at home with him. Last summer he was yachting on the west coast of Scotland, and he described the sunset over the Skye hills; and I tried to give him a Devonshire sunrise. We both forgot where we were, and then Mrs. Chatterby asked me quite loud, so that every one looked, what I thought of 'Smudges.'.

"The dinner table seemed to wait for my answer, and I wish that the book had never come from the library, but I said that I had sent it back because it seemed so bitter and cruel, and one ought to read books which showed the noble side of life.

"'You are one of the old-fashioned women,' she replied. 'You believe in a novel for the young person,' with a smile that hurt me, and I told her that I had been brought up on Sir Walter Scott. I was trying to say something about his purity and chivalry, when I caught Mr. Fynical's eye, and blushed red. If I had only been silent,—for I'm afraid every one was laughing, and Edward did not say one word to me all the way home.

"February 20. Another ordeal, but not so unfortunate as the last. The Browne-Smythes are very kind friends, but I do think they are too much concerned about having clever people at their house. One evening Mrs. Browne-Smythe said she was happy because nothing had been talked about except translations of Homer. A certain guest was so miserable on that occasion that I begged Edward to leave me at home this time, but he said it would not be Greek again. It was science, however, and when we came in Mrs. Browne-Smythe was telling a very learned-looking person that she simply lived for fossils. A young lady beside me was talking about gases to a nervous man, who grew quite red, and tried to escape behind a table. I think she was wrong in her words, and he was too polite to correct her. To my horror, he was obliged to take me in to dinner, and there never could have been two people more deserving of pity, for I was terrified of his knowledge, and he was afraid of my ignorance. We sat in perfect silence till a fatherly old man, quite like a farmer, on my left, began to talk to me so pleasantly that I described our country people, and was really sorry when the ladies had to leave. Edward says that he is one of the greatest discoverers in the world, and has all kinds of honours. We became so friendly that he has promised to take tea with me, and I think he does not despise my simplicity. How I long to be cleverer for Edward's sake, for I'm sure he must be ashamed of me among those brilliant women. I cannot blame him: I am proud of my husband.

"May 15. I am quite discouraged, and have resolved never to go to any charitable committee again. Miss Tabitha Primmer used shameful language at the Magdalene meeting to-day, and Mrs. Wood-Ruler showed me that I had broken Law 43 by giving a poor girl personal aid. It seems presumptuous on my part to criticise such able and diligent workers, but my mother never spoke about certain subjects, and it is agony for me to discuss them. When the vicar insisted on Sunday that thoughtful women were required for Christian service to-day, and that we must read up all kinds of books and know all kinds of painful things, my heart sank. It does not seem as if there was any place left for simple folk like me. Perhaps it would be better to give up going out altogether, and live for Edward and Bertie. I can always do something for them, and their love will be enough reward.

"Nov. 30. I have not slept all night, for I made a dreadful mistake about a new book that every one is reading, and Edward was so angry. He did not mean all he said, but he never called me a fool before. Perhaps he is right, and it is hard on him, who is so bright. Sometimes I wish——" And then there was no writing, only a tear mark. . . .

Afterwards he opened the letters that had come since her death, and this is what he read:

"MY DEAR TREVOR,—

"The intelligence of Mrs. Trevor's death has given me a great shock of regret, and you will allow me to express my sympathy. Many men not given to enthusiasm had told me of her face and goodness, and before I had seen your wife I knew she was a very perfect type of womanliness. The few times I met her, Mrs. Trevor cast a certain spell over me—the nameless grace of the former days—and I felt myself unworthy in her presence. Once when a silly woman referred to one of the most miserable examples of decadent fiction, your wife spoke so nobly of true literature that I was

moved to thank her, but I gathered from her face that this would not be acceptable. It seemed to me that the mask had fallen from a beautiful soul, and one man at least, in whom there is too little reverence, took the shoes from off his feet. Pardon me if I have exceeded, and
   "Believe me,
    "Yours faithfully,
     "BERNARD FYNICAL."

The next was from the F.R.S.

"MY DEAR SIR,—
"It is quite wrong for me, a stranger, to intrude on your grief, but I am compelled to tell you that an old fellow who only spoke to your wife once, had to wipe his spectacles over the *Times* this morning. It came about this way. The lady I had taken in to dinner at the Browne-Smythes gabbled about science till I lost my temper, and told her it would be a good thing if women would keep to their own sphere. Your wife was on the other side, and I turned to her in despair. She delighted me by confessing utter ignorance of my subject, and then she won my heart by some of the loveliest stories of peasant life in Devonshire I ever heard, so full of insight and delicacy. If the parsons preached like that I would be in church next Sunday. She put me in mind of a sister I lost long ago—who had the same low, soft voice and honest,

trusty eyes. When she found I was a lonely man, your wife had pity on me, and asked me to call on her. But I had to go to America, and only returned two days ago. I intended to wish her a Happy New Year, but it's too late. I cannot get you out of my mind, and I thought it might comfort you to know how a fossil like myself was melted by that kind heart.
"Believe me, my dear sir,
"Your obedient servant,
"ARCHIBALD GILMORE."

The third was also from a man, but this time a lad in rooms whom Trevor had seen at the house.

"DEAR MR. TREVOR,—
"You perhaps know that Mrs. Trevor allowed me to spend an hour with her of an evening, when I felt downhearted or had any trouble, but no one will ever know how much she did for me. When I came up to London my faith began to go, and I saw that in a short time I would be an Agnostic. This did not trouble me so much on my own account as my mother's, who is dead, and made me promise something on her death-bed. So I bought books and heard sermons on unbelief till I was quite sick of the whole business. Mrs. Trevor took me to hear your own clergyman, who did not help me one bit, for he was too clever and logical; but you remember I came home with you, and after you

had gone to your study I told Mrs. Trevor my difficulties, and she did me more good than all the books. She never argued nor preached, but when I was with her one felt that religion was a reality, and that she knew more about it than any one I had met since I lost my mother. It is a shame to trouble you with my story when you are in such sorrow, and no one need tell you how noble a woman Mrs. Trevor was; but I could not help letting you know that her goodness has saved one young fellow at least from infidelity and worse.

"You will not mind my having sent a cross to put on the coffin; it was all I could do.

"Yours gratefully,
"GEORGE BENSON."

There was neither beginning nor end to the fourth letter, but it was written in a lady's hand.

"I am a clergyman's daughter, who left her father's house, and went astray. I have been in the Inferno, and have seen what I read in *Dante* while I was innocent. One day the old rectory rose up before my eyes—the roses hanging over my bedroom window; the birds flying in and out the ivy; my father on the lawn, aged and broken through my sin—and I resolved that my womanhood should no longer be dragged in the mire. My home was closed years ago, I had no friends, so I went in my desperation to a certain Institute, and told my case

AFTERWARDS

to a matron. She was not unkindly, but the committee were awful, without either sympathy or manners; and when an unmarried woman wished to pry into the details of my degradation—but I can't tell a man the shame they would have put upon me—my heart turned to flint, and I left the place. I would have gone back to my life and perished had it not been for one woman who followed me out, and asked me to go home with her for afternoon tea. Had she said one word about my past, I had flung myself away; but because she spoke to me as if I were still in the rectory, I could not refuse. Mrs. Trevor never once mentioned my sin, and she saved my soul. I am now a nurse in one of the hospitals, and full of peace. As long as I live I shall lay white flowers on her grave, who surely was the wisest and tenderest of women."

Trevor's fortitude was failing fast before this weight of unconscious condemnation, and he was only able to read one more—an amazing production, that had cost the writer great pains.

"HONOURED SIR,—

"Bill says as it's tyking too much on the likes o' me to be addressing you on your missus' death, but it's not her husband that will despise a pore working woman oo's lost her best friend. When Bill 'ad the rumatiks, and couldn't do no work, and Byby was a-growing that thin you could see

thro' 'im, Mrs. Byles says to me, ' Mrs. 'Awkes, you
goes to the Society for the Horganisation of Female
Toilers.' Says I, ' Wot is that?' and she declares,
' It's a set of ladies oo wants to 'elp women to work,
and they 'ill see you gets it.' So I goes, and I saw
a set of ladies sitting at a table, and they looks at
me; and one with spectacles, and a vice like an 'and-
saw, arsks me, ' Wot's yer name?' and ' 'Ow old
are you?' and ' 'Ow many children have
you?' and ' Are your 'abits temperate?' And
then she says, ' If you pay a shilling we 'ill put your
nyme down for work has an unskilled worker.' ' I
'avn't got a shilling, and Byby's dyin' for want of
food.' ' This ain't a poor 'ouse,' says she; ' this is a
Booro.' When I wos a-going down the stairs, a
lady comes after me. ' Don't cry, Mrs. 'Awkes,'
for she had picked up my name. ' I've some char-
ring for you, and we 'ill go to get something for
Byby.' If ever there wos a hangel in a sealskin
jacket and a plain little bonnet, but the true lady hall
hover, 'er name was Mrs. Trevor. Bill, he looked
up from that day, and wos on his keb in a week,
and little Jim is the biggest byby in the court. Mrs.
Trevor never rested till I got three hoffices to clean,
to say nothing of 'elping at cleanings and parties in
'ouses. She wos that kind, too, and free, when
she'd come hin with noos of some hoffice. ' We're
horganisin' you, Missus 'Awkes, just splendid,' with
the prettiest bit smile. Bill, he used to say, ' 'Er
'usband's a proud man, for I never saw the like o'

her for a downright lady in 'er wys '—and 'e knows, does Bill, being a kebman. When I told 'im, he wos that bad that 'e never put a match to 'is pipe the 'ole night. ' Mariar,' 'e says to me, ' you an' me 'as seen somethink of her, but you bet nobody knew what a saint she wos 'xcept 'er 'usband.' " . . .

Trevor could read no more, for it had dawned at last upon him that Christ had lived with him for more than ten years, and his eyes had been holden.

THE MINISTER OF ST. BEDE'S

THE MINISTER OF ST. BEDE'S

I

It was in the sixties that a southern distiller, who had grown rich through owning many public-houses and much selling of bad gin, bought Glenalder from its poverty-stricken laird, and cleared out the last of the Macdonalds from Lochaber. They arose and departed on a fine spring day, when the buds were bursting on the trees, and the thorn was white as snow, and the birds were bringing forth their young, and the heather was beginning to bloom. Early in the morning, while the grass was yet wet with dew and the sun had not come over the hill, Ian Dhu, at the head of the Glen, with his brothers and their families, their sons and their sons' wives, began the procession, which flowed as a stream of sorrow by the side of the Alder, all the day, gathering its rivulets from every forsaken home. When it reached the poor little clachan, where were the kirk and the graveyard, the emigrants halted, and leaving their goods upon the road went in to worship God for the last time in

Glenalder kirk. A very humble sanctuary, with earthen floor and bare benches, and mightily despised by the kind of southern who visited the new laird's mansion, but beautiful and holy to those who had been baptised there, and married there, and sat with their heart's love there, and who, in that place, but after many years and in old age, had received the sacrament. When they were all in their places, the minister of the Glen, who would fain have gone with them, but was now too old, ascended the pulpit and spake to them from the words, "He went out, not knowing whither he went," charging them never to forget their native country nor their fathers' faith, beseeching them to trust in God and do righteousness, calling them all kinds of tender names in the warm Gaelic speech, till they fell a-weeping, men and women together, and the place was full of lamentation. After which Alister Macdonald, who had been through the Crimean War and the Mutiny, and now was a catechist great in opening mysteries, committed them to the care of their fathers' God. They would hardly leave the kirk, and the sun was westering fast when they came to the elbow of the hill where the traveller gets his last look of the Glen. There they sang, "If I forget thee, O Jerusalem, let my right hand forget her cunning," but it was Glenalder they meant, a parcel of whose earth each family carried with them into exile; and as the pipes played "Lochaber no more" they went away for ever from the land they loved and which had cast them forth. For an hour the minister and Alister, with a handful of old people, watched their kinsfolk till they could see them no more, and then they went back, no one speaking with his neighbour, to the empty Glen.

Besides the huge staring castle, with its lodges, built by the foreigner, there are only some twenty houses now in all bonnie Glenalder. Tourists venturing from the main road come, here and there, across a little heap of stones and the remains of a garden, with some patches of bright green still visible among the heather. It is the memorial of a home where generation after generation of well-built, clean-blooded, God-fearing Highland folk were raised. From those humble cottages went up morning and evening the psalm of praise to God. From them also came hardy men to fill the ranks of the Highland regiments, who had tasted none of the city vices and did not know what fear was. Nor were they a fierce or morose people, for the Glen sounded of a summer evening with the sound of the pipes, playing reels and strathspeys, and in the winter time the minister would lend his barn for a dance, saying, like the shrewd man he was, " The more dancing the less drinking." The very names of those desolate homesteads and the people that lived therein are now passing out of mind in Glenalder, but away in North-West Canada there is a new Glenalder, where every name has been reproduced, and the cuttings of the brier roses bloom

every year in memory of the land that is " far awa."
And if any man from Lochaber, or for that matter
from any part of Scotland, lights on this place, it
will be hard for him to get away from the warm
hearts that are there, and he must depart a better
man after hearing the kindly speech and seeing the
sword dance once more.

While the exiles halted on the elbow of the hill,
each man, woman and child, according to his size
and strength, carried a stone from the hillside and
placed it on a heap that grew before their eyes,
till it made a rough pyramid. This was called the
Cairn of Remembrance, and as often as any one of
the scanty remnant left the Glen to go south it was
a custom that his friends should accompany him
to this spot and bid him farewell, where the past
pledged him to love and faithfulness. It was here
therefore that Henry Rutherford parted from Magdalen Macdonald as he went to his last session at the
Divinity Hall.

"It's four years since I came first to Glenalder
to teach the school in the summer-time, Magdalen,
an' little I thought then I would ever be so near
the ministry or win my sweetheart in the Glen."

They were sitting on a heather bank below the
cairn, and as he spoke his arm slipped round her
waist. He was a typical Scot, with bony frame,
broad shoulders, strong face, deep-set eyes of grey,
and the somewhat assertive and self-sufficient manner of his race. She was of the finest type of High-

land beauty with an almost perfect Grecian face, fair hair dashed with gold, eyes of the blue of the Highland lochs, and a queenly carriage of head and body. Deep-bosomed and unfettered by fashionable city dress, with strong hand and firm foot, she had the swinging gait and proud independence of the free hill woman.

"Had it not been for you," he went on, "I had never persevered; it was your faith put strength in me and hope, and then . . . the help you gave me; I can never forget or repay you. To think that you should have slaved that I should have books and—better food."

"Hush, I command you, for I will not be hearing another word, and if you are saying more I will be very angry. It is not good that any man should be a minister and not keep his word. And the day I gave you the purse with the two or three pieces of gold you made a promise never to speak about that day again. It is not many quarrels we have had, Henry, and some will be good quarrels, for afterward we were loving each other more than ever. But it was not good when you would lay the bits of gold on that very stone there—for I am seeing them lie in the hollow—and say hot words to me."

"Magdalen, I put the purse itself in my breast, and I loved you more than ever for your thought of me and your sacrifice, and I wanted to kiss you, and . . . you ordered me to stand off, and your eyes were blazing. Lassie, you looked like a tigress; I was feared of you."

"It was not for me to have my gifts given back, and if I was driving home the cows and milking the white milk into the pail, and churning the sweet yellow butter, all that my love should not be wanting anything, it is not for him to be so proud and mighty."

"But I did take your kindness at last, and it was more than two or three pounds, and so it was you that sent me to Germany. You gave me my learning, and some day, when we're in our manse together, I'll show you all my books and try . . . to repay your love."

"Henry, it will come over me at times in the twilight, when strange sights are seen, that we shall never be together in our house. Oh, yes, I have seen a room with books round the walls, and you will be sitting there, but I am not seeing any Magdalen. Wait a minute, for there will be another sight, and I am not understanding it. It is not this land, but where it will be I do not know; but I will be there in a beautiful room, and I will be in rich dress, but I am not seeing you.

"Do not speak." She rose up and looked at Rutherford, holding him at arm's length, with her hand upon his shoulder. "Have you got the broken piece?" He thrust his hand into his breast, and showed the jagged half of a common penny hung round his neck by a blue ribbon.

ST. BEDE'S 43

"My half will be here"—Magdalen touched her bosom—"but maybe it will be better for me to give you it, and then . . . you will be free; each of us . . . must drink the cup that is mixed. The visions will be very clear, though I have not the second sight."

"What is the meaning of all this talk, Magdalen?" Rutherford's face was pale, and his voice vibrated. "Are you tired of me because I am not bonnie of face, but only a plain Scot, or is it that you will not wait till I win a home for you, or have you seen another man—some glib English sportsman?"

"God forgive you, Henry Rutherford, for saying such words; is it Alister Macdonald's granddaughter that would play her lover false? Then let him drive the skean dhu into her heart."

"Then it is me you suspect, and it is not what I have deserved at your hands, Magdalen. A Scot may seem cold and hard, but he can be 'siccar,' and if I keep not my troth with you, and deal not by you as you have by me, then may God be my judge and do unto me as I have done unto you."

They looked into one another's eyes, and then tears put out the fire in hers, and she spoke with a wail in her voice.

"This is all very foolish talk, and it is this girl that will be sorry after you are gone and I am sitting lonely, watching the sun go down. But it was a thought that would be coming over my mind, for you will be remembering that I am a Highlander; but it is not that you will not be faithful to me or I to you, oh, no, and I have put it away, my love. Now may God be keeping you "—and she took his hand—" and prospering you in all your work, till you have your heart's desire in knowledge and everything . . . that would be good for you. This is the prayer Magdalen Macdonald will be offering for you every morning and night and all the day when it is winter-time and the snow is heavy in Glenalder."

Then she kissed him full upon the lips as in a sacrament, and looking back he saw her standing against the evening light, the perfect figure of a woman, and she waved to him, whom he was not to see again for ten long years.

II

"Just ventured to look in for a single minute, Mr. Rutherford, at the close of this eventful day, to say how thankful we all are that you were so wonderfully sustained. But you are busy—making notes for next Sabbath, perhaps—and I must not interrupt you. We must keep ourselves open to the light; in my small way I find there are times when the thoughts just drop upon one. If we were more lifted above the world they would come oftener, far oftener."

A very "sleekit" personage indeed, as they say in Scotland, with a suave manner, a sickly voice, and ways so childish that simple people thought him almost silly; but those who happened to have had deals with him in business formed quite another opinion, and expressed it in language bordering on the libellous.

"Will you be seated?" Rutherford laid aside a letter beginning "Dearest Magdalen," and telling how it had fared with him on his first Sunday in St. Bede's, Glasgow, W., a kirk which contained many rich people and thought not a little of itself. "You have a meeting on Sunday evening, I think you said. I hope it was successful."

"There was blessing to-night, I am sure. I felt the power myself. Lord Dunderhead was passing through Glasgow and gave the address. It was on 'The Badgers' Skins' of the Tabernacle, and was very helpful. And afterward we had a delightful little 'sing.' You know his lordship?"

"No, I never saw him," said Rutherford shortly, with a Scot's democratic prejudice against religious snobbery, forgetting that people who will not listen to a reasoned discourse from a clergyman will crowd to the simplest utterance of a lord.

"You will allow me to introduce you on Tuesday evening; you got Mrs. Thompson's card. I hope we may have a profitable gathering. Captain Footyl, the hussar evangelist, will also be present —a truly delightful and devoted young man."

Rutherford had not forgotten the card—

Mr. and Mrs. Thompson
At Home
Tuesday, May 2nd
To meet Lord Dunderhead, who will give
a Bible Reading.

8 to 10.30.   Evening Dress.

And had sent it off to his college friend, Carmichael of Drumtochty, with a running commentary of a very piquant character.

"Thank you, but I fear that my work will prevent me being with you on Tuesday; it is no light thing for a man to come straight from college to St. Bede's without even a holiday."

"So sorry, but by-and-bye you will come to one of our little meetings. Mrs. Thompson greatly enjoyed your sermon to young men this afternoon; perhaps just a little too much of works and too little of faith. Excuse the hint—you know the danger of the day—all life, life; but that's a misleading test. By the way, we are all hoping that you may get settled in a home as well as in your church," continued Mr. Thompson, with pious waggery, and then chilling at the want of sympathy on the minister's face; "but that is a serious matter, and we trust you may be wisely guided. A suitable helpmeet is a precious gift."

"Perhaps you may not have heard, Mr. Thompson, that I am engaged"—and Rutherford eyed the elder keenly,—" and to a girl of whom any man and any congregation may be proud. I am going north next week to see her and to settle our marriage day."

"I am so pleased to hear you say so, and so will all the elders be, for I must tell you that a rumour came to our ears that gave us great concern; but I said we must not give heed to gossip, for what Christian has not suffered in this way at the hand of the world?"

"What was the gossip?" demanded Rutherford,

and there was that in his tone that brooked no trifling.

"You must not take this to heart, dear Mr. Rutherford; it only shows how we ought to set a watch upon our lips. Well—that you were to marry a young woman in Glen—Glen——"

"Alder. Go on," said Rutherford.

"Yes, in Glenalder, where we all rejoice to know you did so good a work."

"I taught a dozen children in the summer months to eke out my living. But about the young woman—what did they say of her?"

"Nothing at all, except that she was, perhaps, hardly in that position of society that a clergyman's wife ought to be, especially one in the west end of Glasgow. But do not let us say anything more of the matter; it just shows how the great enemy is ever trying to create dissension and injure the work."

"What you have heard is perfectly true, except that absurd reference to Glasgow, and I have the honour to inform you, as I intend to inform the elders on my return next week, that I hope to be married in a month or two to Magdalen Macdonald, who was brought up by her grandfather, Alister Macdonald of the Black Watch, and who herself has a little croft in Glenalder "—and Rutherford challenged Mr. Thompson, expounder of scripture and speculator in iron, to come on and do his worst.

ST. BEDE'S

"Will you allow me, my dear young friend, to say that there is no necessity for this . . . heat, and to speak with you as one who has your . . . best interests at heart, and those of St. Bede's. I feel it to be a special providence that I should have called this evening."

"Well?" insisted Rutherford.

"What I feel, and I have no doubt you will agree with me, is that Christians must not set themselves against the arrangements of Providence, and you see we are set in classes for a wise purpose. We are all equal before God, neither 'bond nor free,' as it runs, but it is expedient that the minister of St. Bede's should marry in his own position. There are many sacrifices we must make for our work's sake; and, oh, Mr. Rutherford, what care we have to take lest we cast a stumbling-block in the way of others! It was only last week that a valued fellow-worker begged me to invite a young lady to my little drawing-room meeting who was concerned about spiritual things. 'Nothing would give me greater pleasure,' I said, 'if it would help her; but it is quite impossible, and you would not have asked me had you known her history. Her father was a shopkeeper, and in the present divided state of society I dare not introduce her among the others, all wholesale without exception.' You will not misunderstand me, Mr. Rutherford?"

"You have stated the case admirably, Mr. Thompson, and from your standpoint in religion,

I think, conclusively. Perhaps the Sermon on the Mount might . . . ; but we won't go into that. Before deciding, however, what is my duty, always with your aid, you might like to see the face of my betrothed. There, in that light."

"Really quite beautiful, and I can easily understand; we were all young once and . . . impressionable. As good-looking as any woman in St. Bede's? Excuse me, that is hardly a question to discuss. Grace does not go with looks. We all know that beauty is deceitful. Knows the poets better than you do, I dare say. There is a nurse of my sister's, a cabman's daughter—I beg your pardon for dropping the photograph; you startled me. But you will excuse me saying that it is not this kind of knowledge . . . well, culture, which fits a woman to be a minister's wife. Addressing a mothers' meeting is far more important than reading poetry. Highland manners more graceful than Glasgow? That is a very extraordinary comparison, and . . . can do no good. Really no one can sympathise with you more than I do, but I am quite clear as to your duty as a minister of the Gospel."

"You mean "—and Rutherford spoke with much calmness—" that I ought to break our troth. It is not a light thing to do, sir, and has exposed both men and women to severe . . . criticism."

"Certainly, if the matter be mismanaged, but I think, although it's not for me to boast, that it could be arranged. Now, there was Dr. Drummer—this is quite between ourselves—he involved himself with a teacher of quite humble rank during his student days, and it was pointed out to him very faithfully by his elders that such a union would injure his prospects. He made it a matter of prayer, and he wrote a beautiful letter to her, and she saw the matter in the right light, and you know what a ministry his has been. His present wife has been a real helpmeet; her means are large and are all consecrated."

"Do you happen to know what became of the teacher? I only ask for curiosity, for I know what has become of Dr. Drummer."

"She went to England and caught some fever, or maybe it was consumption, but at any rate she died just before the Doctor married. It was all ordered for the best, so that there were no complications."

"Exactly; that is evident, and my way seems now much clearer. There is just one question more I should like to ask. If you can answer it I shall have no hesitation about my course. Suppose a woman loved a man and believed in him, and encouraged him through his hard college days, and they both were looking forward with one heart to their wedding day, and then he—did not marry her—what would honourable men think of him, and what effect would this deed of —prudence have on his ministry of the Gospel?"

"My dear friend, if it were known that he had taken this step simply and solely for the good of the cause he had at heart and after prayerful consideration, there is no earnest man—and we need not care for the world—who would not appreciate his sacrifice."

"I do not believe one word you say." Mr. Thompson smiled feebly, and began to retire to the door at the look in Rutherford's eye. "But whether you be right or wrong about the world in which you move, I do not know. In my judgment, the man who acted as you describe would have only one rival in history, and that would be Judas Iscariot."

III

Southern travellers wandering over Scotland in their simplicity have a dim perception that the Scot and the Celt are not of one kind, and, as all racial characteristics go back to the land, they might be helped by considering the unlikeness between a holding in Fife and a croft in a western glen. The lowland farm stands amid its neighbours along the highway, with square fields, trim fences, slated houses, cultivated after the most scientific method, and to the last inch a very type of a shrewd, thrifty, utilitarian people. The Highland farm is half a dozen patches of as many shapes scattered along the hillside, wherever there are fewest stones and deepest soil and no bog, and those the crofter tills as best he can—sometimes getting a harvest and sometimes seeing the first snow cover his oats in the sheaf, sometimes building a rude dyke to keep off the big, brown, hairy cattle that come down to have a taste of the sweet green corn, but often finding it best to let his barefooted children be a fence by day, and at certain seasons to sit up all night himself to guard his scanty harvest from the forays of the red deer. Somewhere among the patches he builds his low-roofed house, and thatches it over with straw, on which, by-and-bye, grass with heather and wild flowers begin to grow, till it is not easy to tell his home from the hill. His farm is but a group of tiny islands amid a sea of heather that is ever threatening to overwhelm them with purple spray. Any one can understand that this man will be unpractical, dreamy, enthusiastic, the child of the past, the hero of hopeless causes, the seer of visions.

Magdalen had milked her cows at midday and sent them forth to pasture, and now was sitting before her cottage among wallflower and spring lilies, reading for the third time the conclusion of Rutherford's last letter:—

"Here I was interrupted by the coming of an elder, a mighty man in the religious world, and very powerful in St. Bede's. He tells me that something has been heard of our engagement, and I have taken counsel with him with the result that it seems best we should be married without delay. After loving for four years and there being nothing to hinder, why should you be lonely on your croft in Glenalder and I in my rooms at Glasgow? Answer me that, 'calf of my heart' (I do not attempt the Gaelic). But you cannot. You will only kiss the letter, since I am not at your side, and next week I shall come north, and you will fix the day.

"My head is full of plans, and I do not think

ST. BEDE'S 55

that joy will let me sleep to-night for thinking of you and all that we shall do together. We'll be married early in the morning in the old kirk of Glenalder, as soon as the sun has filled the Glen and Nature has just awaked from sleep. Mona Macdonald will be your bridesmaid, I know, and she will wear white roses that shall not be whiter than her teeth. Yes, I have learned to notice all beautiful things since I knew you, Magdalen. My best man will be Carmichael of Drumtochty, who is of Highland blood himself and a goodly man to look upon, and he has his own love-story. All the Glen will come to our wedding, and will grudge that a Lowland Scot has spoiled the Glen of the Flower of Dalnabreck—yes, I know what they call you. And we shall have our breakfast in the manse, for the minister has pledged us to that, and it is he and John Carmichael that will be making the wonderful speeches! (You see how I've learned the style.) But you and I will leave them and catch the steamer, and then all the long June day we shall sit on the deck together and see distant Skye, and the little isles, and pass Mull and Ardnamurchan, and sail through Oban Bay and down Loch Fyne, and thread our way by Tighnabruaich, and come into the Firth of Clyde when the sun is going down away behind Ben Alder. Won't it be a glorious marriage day, among lochs and hills and islands the like of which travellers say cannot be found in all the world?

"Then I want to take you to Germany, and to show you the old University town where I lived one summer, and we will have one good day there, too, my bride and I. Early in the morning we shall stand in the market-place, where the women are washing clothes at the fountain and the peasants are selling butter and fruit, and the high-gabled houses rise on three sides, and the old Rathhaus, on whose roof the storks build their nests, makes the fourth. We'll go to my rooms near the Kirche, where I used to write a letter to you every day, and here is what old Frau Hepzäcker will say, 'Mein Gott, der Schottlander und ein wunderschönes mädchen' (you will English and Gaelic this for yourself), and we will drink a glass of (fearfully sour) wine with her, and go out with her blessing echoing down the street. Then we will watch the rafts coming down the Neckar from the Black Forest, and walk among the trees in the Vorstadt, where I lay and dreamed of you far away in Glenalder. And we will go to the University where you sent me . . . but that is never to be mentioned again; and the students in their wonderful dress will come and go—red hats and blue, besides the white, black and gold I used to wear. And in the evening we will drive through the vines and fruit-trees to Bebenhausen, the king's hunting-seat. And those will only be two days out of our honeymoon, Magdalen. It seems too good to be my lot that I should be minister of Christ's evangel—of which surely I am not worthy—and that you should be my bride, of which I am as unworthy. Next Monday I shall leave this smoky town and meet you at the Cairn of Remembrance on Tuesday morning.

"Meanwhile and ever I am your faithful lover,
"HENRY RUTHERFORD."

Magdalen kissed the name passionately and thrust the letter into her bosom. Then she went to the edge of the heather and looked along the Glen, where she had been born and lived her twenty-two years in peace, from which she was so soon to go out on the most adventurous journey of life. When a pure-bred Highland woman loves, it is once and for ever, and earth has no more faithful wife, or mother, or daughter. And Magdalen loved Rutherford with all her heart. But it is not given unto her blood to taste unmixed joy, and now she was haunted with a sense of calamity. The past flung its shadow over her, and the people that were gone came back to their deserted homes. She heard the far-off bleating of the sheep and the wild cry of the curlew; she crooned to herself a Gaelic song, and was so carried away that she did not see the stranger come along the track through the heather till he spoke.

"Good evening; may I ask whether this is eh . . . Dalnabreck? and have I the pleasure of addressing Miss Macdonald?"

"Yes, I am Magdalen Macdonald"—and as she faced him in her beauty the visitor was much abashed. "Would you be wanting to see me, sir?"

"My name is Thompson, and I have the privilege of being an elder in St. Bede's, Glasgow, and as I happened to be passing through Glenalder—just a few days' rest after the winter's work—how the soul wears the body!—I thought that it would be . . . a pleasure to . . . pay my respects to one of whom I have . . . heard from our dear pastor. Perhaps, however,"—this with some anxiety—"Mr. Rutherford may have mentioned my humble name."

"There are so many good people in St. Bede's, and they are all so kind to him that . . . Henry"—the flush at her lover's name lent the last attraction to her face and almost overcame the astute iron merchant—"will not be able to tell me all their names. But I will be knowing them all for myself soon, and then I will be going to thank every person for all that has been done to . . . him. It is very gracious of you to be visiting a poor Highland girl, and the road to Dalnabreck is very steep; you will come in and rest in my house, and I will bring you milk to drink. You must be taking care of the door, for it is low, and the windows are small because of the winter storms; but there is room inside and a heart welcome for our friends in our little homes. When I am bringing the milk maybe you will be

ST. BEDE'S

looking at the medals on the wall. They are my grandfather's, who was a brave man and fought well in his day, and two will be my father's, who was killed very young and had not time to get more honour."

The elder made a hurried survey of the room, with its bits of black oak and the arms on the wall, and the deer-skins on the floor, and bookshelves hanging on the wall, and wild flowers everywhere; and, being an operator so keen that he was said to know a market by scent, he changed his plan.

"I took a hundred pounds with me," he explained afterward to a friend of like spirit, "for a promising ministry was not to be hindered for a few pounds! I intended to begin with fifty and expected to bring back twenty-five, but I saw that it would have been inexpedient to offer money to the young woman. There was no flavour of spirituality at all about her, and she was filled with pride about war and such-like vanities. Her manner might be called taking in worldly circles, but it was not exactly . . . gentle, and she might have . . . been rude, quite unpleasant, if I had tried to buy her . . . I mean arrange on a pecuniary basis. Ah, Juitler, how much we need the wisdom of the serpent in this life!"

"What a position you are to occupy, my dear friend," began the simple man, seated before the most perfect of meals—rich milk of cows, fed on meadow grass, yellow butter and white oat cakes set among flowers. "I doubt not that you are often weighed down by a sense of responsibility, and are almost afraid of the work before you. After some slight experience in such matters I am convinced that the position of a minister's wife is the most . . . I may say critical in Christian service."

"You will be meaning that she must be taking great care of her man, and making a beautiful home for him, and keeping away foolish people, and standing by him when his back will be at the wall. Oh, yes, it is a minister that needs to be loved very much, or else he will become stupid and say bitter words, and no one will be wanting to hear him"—and Magdalen looked across the table with joyful confidence.

"Far more than that, I'm afraid"—and Mr. Thompson's face was full of pity. "I was thinking of the public work that falls to a minister's wife in such a church as St. Bede's, which is trying and needs much grace. The receiving of ladies alone —Providence has been very good to our people, twelve carriages some days at the church door— requires much experience and wisdom.

"Mrs. Drummer, who has been much used among the better classes, has often told me that she considered tact in society one of her most precious talents, and I know that it was largely owing to her social gifts, sanctified, of course, that the Doctor became such a power. Ah, yes,"—and Mr. Thompson fell into a soliloquy—" it is the wife that makes or mars the minister."

"Glasgow then will not be like Glenalder"—and Magdalen's face was much troubled—" for if any woman here will tell the truth and speak good words of people, and help when the little children are sick, and have an open door for the stranger, then we will all be loving her, and she will not hurt her man in anything."

" Be thankful that you do not live in a city, Miss Macdonald, for the world has much more power there; they that come to work are in the thick of the battle and need great experience, but you will learn in time and maybe you could live . . . quietly for a year or two . . . you will excuse me speaking like this . . . you see it is for our beloved minister I am anxious."

Magdalen's face had grown white, and she once or twice took a long, sad breath.

" As regards the public work expected of a minister's wife—but I am wearying you, I fear, and it is time to return to the inn. I cannot tell you how much I have enjoyed this delicious milk . . ."

"Will you tell me about the . . . the other things . . . I want to know all."

"Oh, it was the meetings I was thinking of, for of course, as I am sure you know, our minister's wife is the head of the mothers' meeting.

Mrs. Drummer's addresses there were excellent, and her liberality in giving treats—gospel treats, I mean, with tea—was eh, in fact, queenly. And then she had a Bible-class for young ladies that was mentioned in the religious papers."

Magdalen had now risen and was visibly trembling.

"There is a question I would like to ask, Mister . . ."

"Thompson—Jabez Thompson."

"Mister Thompson—and you will be doing a great kindness to a girl that has never been outside Glenalder, and . . . is not wanting to be a sorrow to the man she loves, if you will answer it. Do you know any minister like . . . your minister who married a country girl and . . . what happened?"

"Really, my dear friend, I . . . well, if you insist, our neighbour in St. Thomas's—a very fine young fellow—did, and he was a little hindered at first, but I am sure, in course of time, if he had waited—yes, he left, and I hear is in the Colonies, and doing an excellent work among the squatters, or was it the Chinese? . . . No, no, this is not good-bye. I only hope I have not discouraged you. . . . What a lovely glen! How can we ever make up to you for this heather?"

For three days no one saw Magdalen, but a shepherd attending to his lambs noticed that a lamp burned every night in the cottage at Dalnabreck. When Rutherford arrived at the cairn on Tuesday he looked in vain for Magdalen. Old Elspeth, Magdalen's foster-mother, was waiting for him and placed a letter in his hands, which he read in that very place where he had parted from his betrothed.

"DEAREST OF MY HEART,—

"It is with the tears of my soul that I am writing this letter, and it is with cruel sorrow you will be reading it, for I must tell you that our troth is broken, and that Magdalen cannot be your wife. Do not be thinking this day or any day that she is not loving you, for never have you been so dear to me or been in my eyes so strong and brave and wise and good, and do not be thinking that I do not trust you, for it is this girl knows that you would be true to me although all the world turned against me.

"Believe me, my beloved, it is because I love you so much that I am setting you free that you may not be put to shame because you have married a Highland girl, who has nothing but two cows, and who does not know the ways of cities, and who cannot speak in public places, and who can do nothing except love.

"If it had been possible I would have been waiting for you at the Cairn of Remembrance, and it is my eyes that ache to see you once more, but then I would be weak and could not leave you, as is best for you.

"You will not be seeking after me, for I am going far away, and nobody can tell you where, and this is also best for you and me. But I will be hearing about you, and will be knowing all you do, and there will be none so proud of you as your first love.

"And, Henry, if you meet a good woman and she loves you, then you must not think that I will be angry when you marry her, for this would be selfish and not right. I am going away for your sake, and I will be praying that the sun be ever shining on you and that you become a great man in the land. One thing only I ask—that in those days you sometimes give a thought to Glenalder and your faithful friend,

"Magdalen Macdonald."

IV

"It was a first-rate match, and we were fairly beaten; it was their forward turned the scale. I had two hacks from him myself"—the captain of the Glasgow Football Club nursed the tender spots. "It's a mercy to-morrow's Sunday and one can lie in bed."

"Olive oil is not bad for rubbing. You deserve the rest, old man. It was a stiff fight. By-the-way, I saw Rutherford of St. Bede's there. He cheered like a good 'un when you got that goal. He's the best parson going in Glasgow."

"Can't bear the tribe nor their ways, Charlie, they're such hypocrites, always preaching against the world and that kind of thing and feathering their own nests at every turn. Do you know I calculated that six of them in Glasgow alone have netted a hundred and twenty thousand pounds by successful marriages. That's what sickens a fellow at religion."

"Well, you can't say that against Rutherford, Jack, for he's not married, and works like a coal-heaver. He's the straightest man I've come across either in the pulpit or out of it, besides being a ripping preacher. Suppose you look me up to-morrow about six, and we'll hear what he's got to say."

His friends said that Rutherford was only thirty-four years of age, but he looked as if he were near fifty, for his hair had begun to turn grey, and he carried the traces of twenty years' work upon his face. No one would have asked whether he was handsome, for he had about him an air of sincerity and humanity that at once won your confidence. His subject that evening was the " Sanctifying power of love," and, as his passion gradually increased to white heat, he had the men before him at his mercy. Women of the world complained that he was hard and unsympathetic; some elderly men considered his statements unguarded and even unsound; but men below thirty heard him gladly. This evening he was stirred for some reason to the depths of his being, and was irresistible. When he enlarged on the love of a mother, and charged every son present to repay it by his life and loyalty, a hundred men glared fiercely at the roof, and half of them resolved to write home that very night. As he thundered against lust, the foul counterfeit of love, men's faces whitened, and twice there was a distinct murmur of applause. His great passage, however, came at the close, and concerned the love of a man for a maid: " If it be given to any man in his fresh youth to love a noble woman with all his heart, then in that devotion he shall find an unfail-

ST. BEDE'S 67

ing inspiration of holy thoughts and high endeavours, a strong protection against impure and selfish temptations, a secret comfort amid the contradictions and adversities of life. Let him give this passion full play in his life and it will make a man of him and a good soldier in the great battle. And if it so be that this woman pass from his sight or be beyond his reach, yet in this love itself shall he find his exceeding reward." As he spoke in a low, sweet, intense voice, those in the gallery saw the preacher's left hand tighten on the side of the pulpit till the bones and sinews could be counted, but with his right hand he seemed to hold something that lay on his breast.

"Look here, Charlie"—as the two men stood in a transept till the crowd passed down the main aisle—"if you don't mind I would like . . . to shake hands with the preacher. When a man takes his coat off and does a big thing like that he ought to know that he has . . . helped a fellow."

"I'll go in too, Jack, for he's straightened me, and not for the first time. You know how I used to live . . . well, that is over, and it was Rutherford saved me."

"He looks as if he had been badly hit some time. Do you know his record?"

"There's some story about his being in love with a poor girl, and being determined to marry her, but 'Iron Warrants' got round her and persuaded her that it would be Rutherford's ruin; so she disappeared, and they say Rutherford is waiting for her to this day. But I don't give it as a fact."

"You may be sure every word of it is true, old man; it's like one of Thompson's tricks, for I was in his office once, and it's just what that man in the pulpit would do; poor chap, he's served his time . . . I say, though, suppose that girl turns up some day."

They were near the vestry door and arranging their order of entrance when a woman came swiftly down the empty aisle as from some distant corner of the church and stood behind them for an instant.

"Is this Mr. Rutherford's room, gentlemen"—with a delicate flavour of Highland in the perfect English accent—"and would it be possible for me to see him . . . alone?"

They received a shock of delight on the very sight of her and did instant homage. It was not on account of her magnificent beauty—a woman in the height of her glory—nor the indescribable manner of good society, nor the perfection of her dressing, nor a singular dignity of carriage. They bowed before her for the look in her eyes, the pride of love, and, although both are becoming each day her more devoted slaves, yet they agree that she could only look once as she did that night.

It was Charlie that showed her in, playing beadle for the occasion that this princess might not have to wait one minute, and his honour obliged him to withdraw instantly, but before the door could be closed he heard Rutherford cry—

"At last, Magdalen, my love!"

"Do you think, Charlie . . .?"

"Rutherford has got his reward, Jack, and twenty years would not have been too long to wait."

AN IMPOSSIBLE MAN

AN IMPOSSIBLE MAN

I

"We must have Trixy Marsden on the Thursday,"—for Mrs. Leslie was arranging two dinner parties. "She will be in her element that evening; but what are we to do with Mr. Marsden?"

"Isn't it rather the custom to invite a husband with his wife? he might even expect to be included," said John Leslie. "Do you know I'm glad we came to Putney; spring is lovely in the garden."

"Never mind spring just now," as Leslie threatened an exit to the lawn; "you might have some consideration for an afflicted hostess, and give your mind to the Marsden problem."

"It was Marsden brought spring into my mind," and Leslie sat down with that expression of resignation on his face peculiar to husbands consulted on domestic affairs; "he was telling me this morning in the train that he had just finished a table of trees in the order of their budding, a sort of spring priority list; his love for statistics is amazing.

"He is getting to be known on the 9 train; the men keep their eye on him and bolt into thirds to escape; he gave a morning on the influenza death-rate lately, and that kind of thing spreads.

"But he's not a bad fellow for all that," concluded Leslie; "he's perfectly straight in business, and that is saying something; I rather enjoy half an hour with him."

"Very likely you do," said his wife with impatience, "because your mind has a squint, and you get amusement out of odd people; but every one has not your taste for the tiresome. He is enough to devastate a dinner table; do you remember that escapade of his last year?"

"You mean when he corrected you about the length of the American passage, and gave the sailings of the Atlantic liners since '80," and Leslie lay back to enjoy the past: "it seemed to me most instructive, and every one gave up conversation to listen."

"Because no one could do anything else with that voice booming through the room. I can still hear him: 'the *Columba*, six days, four hours, five minutes.' Then I rose and delivered the table."

"It was only human to be a little nettled by his accuracy; but you ought not to have retreated so soon, for he gave the express trains of England a little later, and hinted at the American lines. One might almost call such a memory genius."

"Which is often another name for idiocy, John. Some one was telling me yesterday that quiet, steady men rush out of the room at the sound of his voice, and their wives have to tell all sorts of falsehoods about their absence.

"Trixy is one of my oldest and dearest friends, and it would be a shame to pass her over; but I will not have her husband on any account."

"Perhaps you are right as a hostess; it is a little hard for a frivolous circle to live up to Marsden, and I hear that he has got up the temperatures of the health resorts; it's a large subject, and lends itself to detail."

"It will not be given in this house. What Trixy must endure with that man! he's simply possessed by a didactic devil, and ought never to have married. Statistics don't amount to cruelty, I suppose, as a ground of divorce?"

"Hardly as yet; by-and-by incompatibility in politics or fiction will be admitted; but how do you know, Florence, that Mrs. Marsden does not appreciate her husband? You never can tell what a woman sees in a man. Perhaps this woman hungers for statistics as a make-weight. She is very amusing, but a trifle shallow, don't you think?"

"She used to be the brightest and most charming girl in our set, and I have always believed that she was married to Mr. Marsden by her people. Trixy has six hundred a year settled on her, and they were afraid of fortune-hunters. Mothers are apt to feel that a girl is safe with a man of the Marsden type, and that nothing more can be desired."

"Perhaps they are not far wrong. Marsden is not a romantic figure, and he is scarcely what you would call a brilliant *raconteur;* but he serves his wife like a slave, and he will never give her a sore heart."

"Do you think it nothing, John, that a woman with ideals should be tied to a bore all her days? What a contrast between her brother and her husband, for instance. Godfrey is decidedly one of the most charming men I ever met."

"He has a nice tenor voice, I grant, and his drawing-room comedies are very amusing. Of course, no one believes a word he says, and I think that he has never got a discharge from his last bankruptcy; but you can't expect perfection. Character seems to oscillate between dulness and dishonesty."

"Don't talk nonsense for the sake of alliteration, John. Trixy's brother was never intended for business; he ought to have been a writer, and I know he was asked to join the staff of the *Boomeller.* Happy thought! I'll ask him to come with his sister instead of Mr. Marsden."

And this was the note:

"MY DEAR TRIXY,—

"We are making up a dinner party for the evening of June 2nd, at eight o'clock, and we simply cannot go on without you and Mr. Marsden. Write

instantly to say you accept; it is an age since I've seen you, and my husband is absolutely devoted to Mr. Marsden. He was telling me only a minute ago that one reason why he goes by the 9 train is to get the benefit of your husband's conversation. With much love,
"Yours affectionately,
"FLORENCE LESLIE.

"P.S.—It does seem a shame that Mr. Marsden should have to waste an evening on a set of stupid people, and if he can't tear himself from his books, then you will take home a scolding to him from me.

"P.S.—If Mr. Marsden *will not* condescend, bring Godfrey to take care of you, and tell him that we shall expect some music."

II

"Come to this corner, Trixy, and let us have a quiet talk before the men arrive from the dining-room. I hope your husband is duly grateful to me for allowing him off this social ordeal. Except perhaps John, I don't think there is a person here fit to discuss things with him."

"Oh, Mr. Marsden does not care one straw whether they know his subjects or not so long as people will listen to him, and I'm sure he was quite eager to come, but I wanted Godfrey to have a little pleasure.

"I'm so sorry for poor Godfrey," and Mrs. Marsden settled herself down to confidences. "You know he lost all his money two years ago through no fault of his own. It was simply the stupidity of his partner, who was quite a common man, and could not carry out Godfrey's plans. My husband might have helped the firm through their difficulty, but he was quite obstinate, and very unkind also. He spoke as if Godfrey had been careless and lazy, when the poor fellow really injured his health and had to go to Brighton for two months to recruit."

"Yes, I remember," put in Mrs. Leslie; "we happened to be at the Metropole one week end, and Godfrey looked utterly jaded."

"You have no idea how much he suffered, Florrie, and how beautifully he bore the trial. Why, had it not been for me, he would not have had money to pay his hotel bill, and that was a dreadful change for a man like him. He has always been very proud, and much petted by people. The poor fellow has never been able to find a suitable post since, although he spends days in the city among his old friends, and I can see how it is telling on him. And —Florrie, I wouldn't mention it to any one except an old friend—Mr. Marsden has not made our house pleasant to poor Godfrey."

"You don't mean that he . . . reflects on his misfortunes."

"Doesn't he? It's simply disgusting what he will say at times. Only yesterday morning—this is absolutely between you and me, one must have some confidant—Godfrey made some remark in fun about the cut of Tom's coat; he will not go, you know, do what I like, to a proper tailor."

"Godfrey is certainly much better dressed," said Mrs. Leslie, "than either of our husbands."

"Perhaps it was that made Tom angry, but at any rate he said quite shortly, 'I can't afford to dress better,' and of course Godfrey knew what he meant. It was cruel in the circumstances, for many men spend far more on their clothes than Godfrey. He simply gives his mind to the matter and takes care of his things; he will spend any time selecting a colour or getting a coat fitted."

"Is your brother quite . . . dependent on . . . his friends, Trixy?"

"Yes, in the meantime, and that is the reason why we ought to be the more considerate. I wished to settle half my income on him, but it is only a third of what it used to be—something to do with investments has reduced it—and Mr. Marsden would not hear of such a thing; he allows Godfrey one hundred a year, but that hardly keeps him in clothes and pocket money."

"Still, don't you think it's all Godfrey could expect?" and Mrs. Leslie was inclined for once to defend this abused man. "Few husbands would do as much for a brother-in-law."

"Oh, of course he does it for my sake, and he means to be kind. But, Florrie, Mr. Marsden is so careful and saving, always speaking as if we were poor and had to lay up for the future, while I know he has a large income and a sure business.

"Why, he would not leave that horrid street in Highbury, say what I could; and I owe it to Godfrey that we have come to Putney. When Tom went out to Alexandria, my brother simply took our present house and had it furnished in Mr. Marsden's name, and so when he came home from Alexandria we were established in The Cottage."

"John is the best of husbands, but I dare not have changed our house in his absence," and Mrs.

Leslie began to get new views on the situation. "Was Mr. Marsden not rather startled?"

"He was inclined to be angry with Godfrey, but I sent the boy off to Scarborough for a month; and he is never hasty to me, only tiresome—you can't imagine how tiresome."

"Is it the statistics?"

"Worse than that. He has begun the Reformation now, and insists on reading from some stuffy old book every evening, *Dumas' History*, I think, till I wish there never had been such a thing, and we were all Roman Catholics."

"Very likely he would have read about the Popes, then, or the saints. My dear girl, you don't wish to have your mind improved. You ought to be proud of your husband; most men sleep after dinner with an evening paper in their hands, and are quite cross if they're wakened. But there they come, and we must have Godfrey's last song."

III

"Nurse will rise at four and bring you a nice cup of tea. Are you sure you will not weary, being alone for two hours?" and Mrs. Marsden, in charming outdoor dress, blew eau-de-Cologne about the room. "Don't you love scent?"

"Where are you going?" asked Marsden, following her with fond eyes. "You told me yesterday, but I forget; this illness has made me stupider than ever, I think. Wasn't it some charity?"

"It's the new society every one is so interested in, 'The Working Wives' Culture Union.' What is wanted is happy homes for the working men," quoting freely from an eloquent woman orator, "and the women must be elevated; so the East End is to be divided into districts, and two young women will be allotted to each. Are you listening?"

"Yes, dear; but it rests me to lie with my eyes closed. Tell me all about your society. What are the young ladies to do?"

"Oh, they're to visit the wives in the afternoon and read books to them: solid books, you know, about wages and . . . all kinds of things working men like. Then in the evening the wives will be able to talk with their husbands on equal terms, and the men will not want to go to the public-houses. Isn't it a capital idea?"

A sad little smile touched Marsden's lips for an instant. "And where do you meet to-day? It's a long way for you to go to Whitechapel."

"Didn't I tell you? The Marchioness of Gloucester is giving a Drawing Room at her town house, and Lady Helen wrote an urgent note, insisting that I should come, even though it were only for an hour, as her mother depended on my advice so much.

"Of course, I know that's just a way of putting it; but I have taken lots of trouble about founding the Union, so I think it would hardly do for me to be absent. You're feeling much better, too, to-day, aren't you, Thomas?"

"Yes, much better; the pain has almost ceased; perhaps it will be quite gone when you return. Can you spare just ten minutes to sit beside me? There is something I have been wanting to say, and perhaps this is my only chance. When I am well again I may . . . be afraid."

Mrs. Marsden sat down wondering, and her husband waited a minute.

"One understands many things that puzzled him before, when he lies in quietness for weeks and takes an after look. I suspected it at times before, but I was a coward and put the thought away. It seemed curious that no one came to spend an hour with me, as men do with friends; and I noticed that they appeared to avoid me. I thought it was fancy, and that I had grown self-conscious.

"Everything is quite plain now, and I . . . am not hurt, dear, and I don't blame any person; that would be very wrong. People might have been far more impatient with me, and might have made my life miserable.

"God gave me a dull mind and a slow tongue; it took me a long time to grasp anything, and no one cared about the subjects that interested me. Beatrice . . . I wish now you had told me how I bored our friends; it would have been a kindness; but never mind that now; you did not like to give me pain.

"What troubles me most is that all these years you should have been tied to a very tiresome fellow," and Marsden made some poor attempt at a smile. "Had I thought of what was before you, I would never have asked you to marry me.

"Don't cry, dear; I did not wish to hurt you. I wanted to ask your pardon for . . . all that martyrdom, and . . . to thank you for . . . being my wife; and there's something else.

"You see when I get well and am not lying in bed here, maybe I could not tell you, so let me explain everything now, and then we need not speak about such things again.

"Perhaps you thought me too economical, but I was saving for a purpose. Your portion has not brought quite so much as it did, and I wished to make it up to you, and now you can have your six hundred a year as before; if this illness had gone against me, you would have been quite comfortable—in money, I mean, dear.

"No, I insist on your going to Lady Gloucester's; the change will do you good, and I'll lie here digesting the Reformation, you know," and he smiled, better this time, quite creditably, in fact. "Will you give me a kiss, just to keep till we meet again?"

When the nurse came down at four to take charge, she was horrified to find her patient alone, and in the death agony, but conscious and able to speak.

"Don't ring . . . nor send for my wife . . . I sent . . . her away knowing the end was near . . . made her go, in fact . . . against her will."

The nurse gave him brandy, and he became stronger for a minute.

"She has had a great deal to bear with me, and I . . . did not wish her to see death. My manner has been always so wearisome . . . I hoped that . . . nobody would be here. You are very kind, nurse; no more, if you please.

"Would it trouble you . . . to hold my hand, nurse? It's a little lonely . . . I am not afraid . . . a wayfaring man . . . though a fool . . . not err therein . . ."

He was not nearly so tedious with his dying as he had been with his living; very shortly afterwards Thomas Marsden had done with statistics for ever.

IV

Three days later Leslie came home from the city with tidings on his face, and he told them to his wife when they were alone that night.

"Marsden's lawyer made an appointment after the funeral, and I had an hour with him. He has asked me to be a trustee with himself in Mrs. Marsden's settlement."

"I'm so glad; you must accept, for it will be such a comfort to poor Beatrice; but I thought Godfrey was her sole trustee."

"So he was," said Leslie, grimly, "more's the pity, and he embezzled every penny of the funds —gambled them away in card-playing and . . . other ways."

"Godfrey Harrison, Beatrice's brother?"

"Yes, her much-admired, accomplished, ill-used brother, the victim of her husband's stinginess."

"If that be true, then Godfrey is simply a . . ."

"You mean an unmitigated scoundrel. Quite so, Florence, and a number of other words we won't go over. I tell you," and Leslie sprang to his feet, "there is some use in swearing; if it had not been for one or two expressions that came to my memory suddenly to-day, I should have been ill. Curious to say, the lawyer seemed to enjoy them as much as myself, so it must be a bad case."

"But I don't understand—if Godfrey spent Trixy's money, how is there anything to manage? Did he pay it back?"

"No, he did not, and could not; he has not enough brains to earn eighteenpence except by cheating, and if by any chance he came into a fortune, would grudge his sister a pound."

"Then . . .?"

"Don't you begin to catch a glimpse of the facts? Why, Marsden toiled and scraped, and in the end, so the doctors say, killed himself to replace the money, and he had just succeeded before his death."

"How good of him! but I don't see the necessity of all this secrecy on his part, and all those stories about low interest that he told Trixy."

"There was no necessity; if it had been some of us, we would have let Mrs. Marsden know what kind of brother she had, and ordered him out of the country on threat of jail.

"It was Marsden's foolishness, let us call it, to spare his wife the disgrace of her idol and the loss of his company. So her husband was despised beside this precious rascal every day."

"Trixy will get a terrible shock when she is told; it would almost have been kinder to let her know the truth before he died."

"Mrs. Marsden is never to know," said Leslie; "that was his wish; she's just to be informed that new trustees have been appointed, and we are to take care that she does not waste her income on the fellow.

"People will send letters of condolence to Mrs. Marsden, but they will say at afternoon teas that it must be a great relief to her, and that it's quite beautiful to see her sorrow. In two years she will marry some well-dressed fool, and they will live on Marsden's money," and Leslie's voice had an unusual bitterness.

"Did you ever hear of another case like this, John?"

"Never; when old Parchment described Marsden giving him the instructions, he stopped suddenly.

"'Marsden,' he said, 'was the biggest fool I ever came across in the course of forty-two years' practice,' and he went over to the window."

"And you?"

"I went to the fireplace; we were both so disgusted with the man that we couldn't speak for five minutes."

After a short while Mrs. Leslie said, "It appears to me that this slow, uninteresting man, whom every one counted a bore, was in his own way . . . almost a hero."

"Or altogether," replied John Leslie.

RIGHTEOUS OVER MUCH

RIGHTEOUS OVER MUCH

I

"How do you do, Crashaw? didn't know you condescended to conversaziones at the Town Hall, at least when there is no dancing. Their Worships will be satisfied this evening, for the whole world and his wife seem to be here, and some people that have never been in the world before, one would judge."

"There is just one person I wish particularly to see, and I can't find her; that is Arkwright's young wife. I passed the old man himself a minute ago, conversing with Peterson, and lecturing on the effect of the American tariff on wool. Has he left her at home, Jack, to keep her out of harm and to tantalise the public?"

"Not he. Jacob is quite proud of her, to do him justice, and worships the ground on which she treads, although I doubt whether she knows that or cares. Mrs. Arkwright is very beautiful in my humble judgment, but there is a wide gulf between twenty-one and seventy. Besides, she has a temper, and no sympathy with his religious notions. When December weds May, it's bound to be either a comedy or a tragedy, and this is half and between."

"When you have quite finished your interesting moral reflections, Jack, and can attend to practical detail, could you do me the pleasure of pointing Mrs. Arkwright out to me, and, as you seem to have seen a good deal of her, introducing your unworthy servant? I'll be able then to judge for myself. We are obliged to Arkwright for creating a piquant situation."

"Come to the next room, where the band is playing; Mrs. Arkwright was there ten minutes ago. But I don't know whether I can intrude on her at the present moment, even although provided with so good-looking and well-dressed an excuse. Yes; there, Crashaw, in the alcove, talking to a parson; that is Jacob's wife. Was I right?"

"Your taste, Jack, is perfect, but, indeed, a man who admires Mrs. Arkwright deserves no credit; it is inevitable. There is prettiness, and there is sweetness, and there is taking-ness, and they are very well, but this is on another level."

"I thought you would be astonished, and am pleased to notice that even so *blasé* a critic of womankind can grow enthusiastic on occasion. Isn't that a proud head?"

"Why, Jack, that woman ought to have been a duchess, and a leader of society in town, instead of Mrs. Jacob Arkwright, wife of a self-made woolspinner and a deacon. Her face is the most complete piece of Grecian beauty I ever saw—nose, eyes, chin, mouth, perfect; forehead perhaps the slightest bit high—a Greek would have worn a ribbon—and that glorious hair, brown shot with gold."

"She is certainly looking splendid to-night. Do you notice how she has put the other women to confusion?"

"Simply a goddess among a lot of peasants. I say, Jack, how in the world did that girl, with such a face and such an air, ever marry Arkwright? Where was she hidden away? Had she no opportunity? Talk about waste, this is an absolute sin. Do you know her history?"

"Lived with her mother, and got her living by teaching. Arkwright, who has all his life been busy with wool and religious affairs, saw her in chapel, and remembered he was human. Fell in love with her on first sight, having lived scatheless unto three score years and ten, and got a fellow-deacon to negotiate the affair; at least, so it is reported."

"Most likely, I should say; but, Jack, what an abandoned criminal that mother of hers must have been, and what did she herself do this thing for? She has a will of her own, or else I do not know a woman's face."

"Oh, the old story. Her mother was proud and poor, and considered Arkwright an excellent suitor. Mrs. Arkwright is not much troubled about religion, and I fancy has a very different idea of things from her husband, but she had the chance of a handsome provision for herself and her mother, and she seized it. There could be no romance; but can you blame the old lady, Crashaw, urging such a marriage, or the daughter escaping from the dreary governess life?"

"No, I suppose not. The girl took the veil, and obtained a settlement at the same time, after a sound Protestant fashion; but it does seem a crime against nature to sacrifice a beautiful young woman to a hard, bloodless old Puritan like Arkwright, who is, I grant you, very able in wool, and perfectly straight in character, but who is perfectly uncultured and hopelessly bigoted. What a life of dreariness she must lead in the Arkwright circle!"

"Well, of course she can't attend concerts, nor dance, nor hunt, nor go into society, but she has a good home, and a carriage, and as much money as she can spend. I don't suppose that she cares for Jacob, but she does her duty as a wife, and does not seem unhappy."

"Certainly Mrs. Arkwright is not unhappy this evening with her present companion. I will hazard the guess, Jack, without any reflection on her wifely character, that she never looked at her worthy, but not very attractive, husband with the same interest which she is bestowing on that handsome parson. Who is he, Jack?"

"Egerton's his name, and he's Arkwright's minister—a Congregationalist, or Baptist; I can never remember the difference. He is a very able fellow, they say, and a rattling good preacher, quite broad and liberal in his views, but a perfect ascetic in his life. He must be very much in Mrs. Arkwright's company, and he's certainly the decentest man she knows."

"Arkwright is about seventy, and is not so strong as he looks, Jack; his wife will have time to console herself, and her second husband will be a very lucky man, for he will have a fortune and her heart."

II

"You have come quickly, Mr. Egerton, and that was well done," said Jacob Arkwright, looking very white and worn, propped up with pillows. "I have much to say, and I'll take a sup o' brandy; them that never touches drink when they're well get the good when they're ill.

"That gives me the strength I need for the time, and ma work is nearly done. Don't go away, Laura; I want you to hear what I say to the pastor.

"The doctor says 'at ma days are few, mayhap only to-morrow, and it's best to speak when a man's head is clear, and I thank God mine is that, though my body be weakened by this sickness."

His wife stood on one side of the bed, now and then rearranging the pillows at his back and bathing his forehead with vinegar—for scent he would not have—and Egerton stood on the other, refusing to sit down while she stood, and watching her strong white hands at their service, but only once did he look her straight in the face.

"You're young, Pastor—thirty, did ye say?—and I'm owd, seventy-two this month, and I havena known you long, but there's no mon I've liked better or could trust more." And he looked steadily at Egerton with a certain softening of expression.

"You've been very kind to me and to the chapel, Mr. Arkwright, and I hope it may be God's will to spare you and raise you up again," and although the words were formal, the accent was tender and moving.

"No, no, lad; our times are in His hand, and I have received the summons, and so we 'ill go to business. And first about ma affairs. I wish ye to understand everything, that ye may be able to do your duty by ma widow."

Egerton was conscious that Mrs. Arkwright straightened herself, and could feel the silence in the room; but the dying man was not one to appreciate an atmosphere.

"It may be that I was too owd for marrying, and ma ways too old-fashioned. Ma house has no been very bright for a young wife, and ma conscience did not allow me liberty in worldly amusements. But according to my nature I can say before God that I loved ye, Laura, and have tried to do ma part by ye."

"You married me a poor girl, and have been most . . . kind to me, Jacob. Why speak of such things?" and her voice was proud and pained.

"You have been a faithful wife to me," he went on, as one fulfilling a plan, "and have put up with my . . . peculiarities—for I know you do not think wi' me in things, and do not like some of the men 'at came to the house. Oh, I said nowt, but I saw aal."

Mrs. Arkwright laid her hand on her husband's, and it occurred to Egerton from a slight flush on his face that she had never done this before.

"Ma will has been made for a year"—it was plain that Mr. Arkwright was to go on to the end, and Egerton could not have lifted his eyes for a ransom—"and I have left aal to my wife without any condition, with just one legacy. It is to you, Egerton, and I hope you 'ill not refuse it—just something to remind you of me, and . . . get you books."

"It was very . . . good of you, sir, and I am most . . . grateful, but I . . . really can't accept your kindness. It is not likely that I will ever marry, and I've got enough for myself."

As he spoke, Mrs. Arkwright shook up the pillows hastily, and went to a side table for a glass.

"Well, if you will not, then there's an end of it; but you will grant me another favour which may be harder," and for a minute Arkwright seemed to hesitate.

"Ma wife will be left young and rich, and although I have never said it to you, ma lass, she is . . . beautiful."

"Jacob, this is not seemly." Her voice was vibrant with passion.

"Blame me not for saying this once, and if another be present, he is our friend, and I am coming to my point; the brandy again, and I'll soon be done.

"You have no brother, and I have no person of my blood to guide you, ma lass; ye might be persecuted by men 'at would bring you nowt but trouble and vexation of heart. You need an honest man to be your guardian and give you advice.

"Ye may never want to marry again, for I doubt ye have had little joy these years, or again ye may, to taste some joy, and I would count it unjust to hinder you—peace, lass, till I be done; I was ever rough and plain—and some one must see that your husband be a right mon.

"So I turned it over in ma mind, and I sought for a friend 'at was sound o' heart and faithful. This speaking is hard on me, but it 'ill soon be done." And as Mrs. Arkwright stooped to give him brandy once more, Egerton saw that her cheeks were burning.

"An older mon might have been better, but ye're old for your years, Pastor, and have parted wi' the foolishness o' youth. You have some notions I don't hold with, for I'm the owd sort—believe and be saved, believe not and be damned—but ye're no a mon to say yea and do nay. Naa, naa, I have seen more than I said; and though some 'at came to the house had the true doctrine, they were shoddy stuff.

"George Egerton, as I have done good to you

and not ill these years, will ye count Laura Arkwright as your sister, and do to her a brother's part, as ye will answer to God at the laast day?"

The wind lifted the blind and rustled in the curtains; the dying man breathed heavily, and waited for an answer. Egerton looked across the bed, but Mrs. Arkwright had withdrawn behind the curtain. Arkwright's eyes met the minister's with an earnest, searching glance.

"I will be as a brother to your wife while I live."

As he spoke, Arkwright grasped his hand and gave a sigh of content; but when Egerton left the room, Laura refused to touch his hand, and her face was blazing with anger.

III

"You have been very generous to the chapel, and we thank you very much for keeping up all Mr. Arkwright's subscriptions those three years. The work of God would have been much crippled had it not been for your liberality."

"Do you know, Mr. Egerton, that when you talk in that grave, approving fashion, as if I were one of your devout women like poor Mrs. Tootle, who is really a good creature, although her husband is a sanctimonious idiot, I feel a perfect hypocrite."

"Why do you always depreciate yourself . . ."

"Do not interrupt me, for I am determined to settle this matter once for all, and not walk about in a vain show, as if I were a saint. You think me good, and so do the chapel people, I suppose, because I give to foreign missions and Bible-women, and go to the prayer-meeting, and attend the special meetings. Do you know why I do those things?"

"Yes, I think so," said the minister; "but I will hear your reason."

"Because Mr. Arkwright believed in missions and evangelists, and he was . . . a better husband to me than I was wife to him, and because it would be dishonourable not to use his money for the objects he approved."

"And the services? Is that the reason you are always present, and set such a good example?" And it was plain the minister did not take Mrs. Arkwright at her value of herself.

"Oh, this is because . . . because . . ."

"Yes?" And Mr. Egerton smiled as one who is giving checkmate.

"Because you were Jacob's friend, and the only man he . . . loved, and because, although we have quarrelled several times, and I have been very rude to you once or twice, still,"—and a smile brought Mrs. Arkwright's face to perfection—"we are friends also."

"You have been . . . angry with me," said Egerton, "when I could not understand the reason, but I never doubted your friendship. If I were in serious trouble, I would come to you rather than to any man."

"Would you really?" Then her tone changed. "I don't believe you, for you would go to some snuffy, maundering old minister."

"And you are good," he insisted, taking no notice of her petulance. "You are honest, and brave, and high-minded, and loyal, and . . ."

"Pious, with a gift of prayer, you had better

add. How blind you are, for all your knowledge and . . . other qualities. You forgot to add sweet-tempered; but perhaps you were coming to that."

"No, I would not say that, and I am rather glad you are not gentle,"—the minister was very bold,—"for you would not be . . . yourself."

"You had your suspicions, then, and are not sure that I am ready for canonising? Do you know I feel immensely relieved; suppose we celebrate this confession by tea? Would you ring the bell, Mr. Egerton?"

"There is something I want to talk about, and as it's rather important, would you mind, Mrs. Arkwright, giving me a few minutes first? Tea is rather distracting."

"Composing, I find it—but as you please; is it the District Visitors, or the Nurses' Home, or the Children's Holiday, and is it money?" Mrs. Arkwright for some reason was very gracious.

"No, it has nothing to do with the chapel. I wish to speak about . . . yourself."

"Yes?" and she looked curiously at him.

"You remember that day when Mr. Arkwright committed you to my care, and I gave my word to . . ."

"Do your best to look after a very troublesome woman," Mrs. Arkwright interposed hurriedly; "it was a . . . risky task, and I thought you were far too hasty, and just a little presumptuous, in undertaking it, but you've been a very lenient guardian for your age. Have I done anything wrong?"

"No, and you could not at any time in my eyes"—Mrs. Arkwright made as though she would curtsey—"but others might do wrong to you, and I have been anxious for some time.

"Mr. Arkwright was afraid lest some unworthy man should admire you or desire your wealth, and . . . marry you, and your life be miserable. And he wished me to save you from this, and I promised to do my best."

"Well?" and her voice had begun to freeze. "I remember all that."

"It is difficult to speak about such things, but you know that I . . . would do anything to save you pain. . . ."

"Go on," and now her eyes were fixed on the minister.

"It came to my ears and I saw for myself that one whom I knew slightly and did not like was paying you attentions, and it might be, as I also heard, was favoured by you. So it seemed my duty to make enquiries about Mr. Crashaw."

"And?"

"There is nothing against his character, and I have heard much good of him—that he has cultured tastes and is very well liked by those who know him; personally we could never be friends, for various reasons, but he . . . is not unworthy to be the husband of . . . a good

RIGHTEOUS OVER MUCH

woman. That is all I have to say"; and the saying of it was plainly very hard to the minister.

"You recommend me to marry Mr. Crashaw, if that gentleman should do me the honour to ask my hand, or do you propose to suggest this step to him, so as to complete your duty as guardian?" Mrs. Arkwright was now standing and regarding Egerton with fierce scorn.

"My information seemed to me reliable"—he was also standing, white and pained—"and I thought it would help you in that case to know what I have told you, when you came to decide."

"If I knew who told you such falsehoods, I would never speak to them again, and I would make them suffer for their words. Mr. Crashaw! and it was to that cynical, worldly, supercilious tailor's block you were to marry me. What ill have I done you?"

"God knows I did not desire. . . . I mean . . . do you not see that I tried to do what was right at a cost? . . . Why be so angry with me?"

"Because I do not really care what any person in this town or all Yorkshire says about me, but I do care and cannot endure that you should turn against me, and be content to see me Crashaw's wife or any other man's." And she drove the minister across the room in her wrath—he had never seen her so beautiful—till he stood with his back to the door, and she before him as a lioness robbed of her cubs.

"It has been my mistake, for I understand not women," he said, with proud humility. "I beg your pardon, and am more than ever . . . your servant."

She looked at him stormily for ten seconds; then she turned away. "If that is all you have to say, you need not come again to this house."

IV

"You will excuse me sending a verbal message by the doctor, for, as you see, I am past writing, and . . . the time is short. I wanted to speak with you, Mrs. Arkwright, once before . . . I died." And Egerton thought of the day she had stood by her husband's deathbed as now she stood by his, only that the nurse had left the room and there was no third person to be an embarrassment.

"Do not suppose I forget your words to me the last time we met in private," he continued, as she did not speak nor look at him, beyond one swift glance as she came into the room; "and believe me, I would not have forced myself on you, nor would I have asked this favour, had it not been that . . . I have something of which I must deliver my soul."

"You are not dying; you were a strong man, and a few days' illness couldn't . . . be fatal," she burst out, and it seemed as if Mrs. Arkwright for once was going to lose control and fall a-weeping. Then she mastered herself, and said almost coldly, "Had I known you were so ill, I would have called to inquire; but nothing was said of pneumonia, only a bad cold."

"You forgive me, then, that ill-judged interference, Mrs. Arkwright, and anything else in which I have offended you or failed in . . . my brother's part?"

"Do not speak like that to me unless you wish to take revenge; it is I who ask your pardon for my evil temper and insolence that day, and other times; but you are too . . . good, else you would have understood."

"You did not, then, hate me, as I supposed?" and his voice was strained with eagerness.

"When you were prepared to approve my engagement to Mr. Crashaw? Yes, I did, and I could have struck you as you bore witness to his character—whom you detested. Conscientious and unselfish . . . on your part, very. And yet at the same time I . . . did not hate you; I could have . . . you are a dull man, Mr. Egerton, and I am not a saint. Is it milk you drink?" And when she raised his head, her hands lingered as they had not done before on her husband's.

"Are you really dying?" She sat down and looked at him, her head between her hands. "You and I are, at least, able to face the situation."

"Yes, without doubt; but I am not a martyr to overwork, or anything else; my death is not a sentimental tragedy; do not let any one speak of me in that fashion: I simply caught a cold and did not take care; it's quite commonplace." When he smiled his face was at its best, the dark blue eyes having a roguish look as of a boy.

Mrs. Arkwright leant back on her chair and bit her lower lip.

"This is good-bye, then, and our friendship—six years long, isn't it?—is over. Had I known it was to be so short—well, we had not quarrelled."

"Not over," and he looked wistfully at her; "this life does not end all."

"Ah, you have the old romantic faith, and one would like to share it, but no one knows; this life is the only certainty."

"In a few hours," he went on, "I shall know, and I expect to see my friend Jacob Arkwright, whom I loved, although we only knew one another for three years, and he . . . will ask for you."

Mrs. Arkwright regarded Egerton with amazement.

"He will ask how I kept my trust, and I . . . will be ashamed, unless you hear my confession and forgive me. For I . . . have sinned against you and your husband."

"In what?" she asked, with a hard voice.

"God knows that I had no thought of you he might not have read while he was here. And afterwards for a year I was in heart your brother; and then—oh, how can I say it and look you in the face, who thought me good and a faithful minister of Christ?" and his eyes were large with pain and sorrow.

"Say it," she whispered, "say it plain; you must," and she stretched out her hand in commandment.

"I loved you as . . . a man loves a woman whom he would make his wife, till it came to pass that I made excuses to visit you, till I watched you on the street, till I longed for the touch of your hand, till I . . . oh, the sin and shame— thought of you in the service and . . . at my prayers; yet I had been left your guardian and had promised to be as a brother to you; besides, nor was this the least of my shame, you were rich."

"And now?" She had risen to her feet.

"I have finally overcome, but only within these few months, and my heart is at last single. You are to me again my friend's wife, and I shall meet him . . . in peace, if you forgive me."

For a few seconds nothing was heard but his rapid breathing, and then she spoke with low, passionate voice.

"Your love needs no forgiveness; your silence . . . I can never forgive."

He lived for two hours, and he spoke twice. Once he thanked his nurse for her attentions, and just before he passed away she caught the words, "through much tribulation . . . enter the Kingdom . . . God."

A PROBATIONER

A PROBATIONER

One winter I forsook the cottage at Drumtochty, in spite of the pure white snow and the snell, bracing wind from Ben Urtach, and took rooms in Edinburgh. It was a poor exchange, for the talk of professors and advocates, although good enough in its way, was not to be compared with the wisdom of James Soutar; but there were more books in Edinburgh than in the Glen, and it was there that I met my probationer. From time to time we passed upon the stair, when he would shrink into a landing and apologise for his obstruction, and if in sheer forgetfulness I said " Fine day," with the rain beating on the windows, he nervously agreed. With his suspicion of clerical attire, and his deferential manner, he suggested some helot of the ecclesiastical world, whose chiefs live in purple and fine linen, and whose subordinates share with tramway men and sempstresses the honour of working harder and receiving less pay than any other body in the commonwealth. By his step I had identified him as the tenant of a single room above my sitting-room, and one wondered how any man could move so little and so gently. If he shifted a chair, it was by stealth, and if in poking his fire a coal dropped on the hearth, he abandoned the audacious attempt.

One grew so accustomed to these mouse-like movements that it came as a shock when my neighbour burst into activity. It was on a Friday afternoon that he seemed to be rearranging his furniture so as to leave a clear passage from end to end of the room, and then, after he had adjusted the chairs and table to his satisfaction, he began a wonderful exercise. Sometimes he would pace swiftly backwards and forwards with a murmuring sound as one repeating passages by rote, with occasional sudden pauses, when he refreshed his memory from some quarter. Sometimes he stood before the table and spoke aloud, rising to a pitch, when one could catch a word or two, and then he would strike a book, quite fiercely for him, and once or twice he stamped his foot almost as hard as a child could. After this outbreak he would rest awhile, and then begin again on the lower key, and one knew when he reached the height by the refrain, "Abana and Pharpar, rivers of Damascus." It was an amazing development, and stimulated thought.

"No," explained our excellent landlady, "he's no daft, though ye micht think sae. He's a minister without a kirk, an' he's juist learnin' his sermon; but, Losh keep us, he's by ordinar' the day.

"He's my cousin's son, ye see"—and Mrs. Macfarlane settled to historical detail—"an' his mother's a weedow. She focht to get him through St. Andrew's, an' hoo she managed passes me. Noo he's what is called a probationer, an', eh, but he earns his livin' hard.

"His business," continued Mrs. Macfarlane, "is to tak' the pulpit when a minister is awa' at a Sacrament or on his holiday, and ae Sabbath he micht be at Peterhead and the next at Wigtown. He gets his orders on Friday, an' he sets aff wi' his bit bag on Saturday, an' a weary body he is on Monday nicht. An' it's little he maks for a' he does, bare twenty shillin' a week clear; but naebody can stand this colie shangle (disturbance)." For above the landlady's exposition rose the probationer's voice: "Abana and Pharpar, rivers of Damascus."

What she said to her cousin once removed I know not, but it was not in vain, for in the evening this was brought by the servant:—

"DEAR SIR,—

"It affords me sincere regret to learn that you have been disturbed in the midst of your literary avocations by sounds and movements emanating from my room. They are unfortunately and unavoidably connected with a new method of professional work which I have been advised to adopt by experienced friends. It would, however, be unrighteous that one man should hinder another in his daily labour, and I would be greatly obliged

if you could indicate any time of absence during which I might be free to speak aloud and move with energy in my chamber without offence. Apologising for my unwitting annoyance,
"I am,
".Yours respectfully,
"HIRAM CLUNAS."

It was written on poor paper and a single sheet, but the handwriting was that of a scholar, a man accustomed to form Hebrew and Greek characters, and the very flavour of pedantry was attractive, so that one wanted to know the writer, and I seized the excuse of a personal answer.

He was quite unprepared for my coming, and upset a Hebrew lexicon and four German books on the Prophets before he could get a chair in his single room below the slates; nor had he any small talk to offer, but he was ready enough to speak about his own work, and seemed anxious to explain his recent departure. It also occurred to me that he wanted my judgment.

"My work, let me explain," he said, hesitatingly, "is not pastoral or . . . devoted to a particular sphere, since my gifts have not yet . . . commended themselves to a congregation after such a fashion that they were inclined to . . . in short, wished to have me as their minister. Mine is a vagum ministerium. I am what is called a probationer, that is, I have been duly educated in profane and sacred learning for the holy ministry, and have passed certain examinations . . . without discredit."

"Of that I am sure," I interpolated with sincerity, whereat the probationer ought to have bowed and replied, "It is very good of you to say so," but as it was he only blushed and looked as if he had been caught boasting.

"And then?" I suggested.

"It remains to discover whether I am . . . fit for the practical work of my calling—if it be, indeed, I am called at all . . ." And here the little man came to a halt.

"You are examined again," I inquired, tentatively, "or placed under a chief for a little?"

"Well, no, although the latter would be an excellent way—but it is not for me to criticise the rules of my Church; if any congregation has lost its minister, then such as I, that is, persons in a state of probation, are sent each Sabbath to . . . preach, and then the people choose the one who . . ." And again Mr. Clunas came to a stand for want of fitting words.

"Who comes out first in the preaching competition," I added, and in an instant was sorry.

"It would ill become me to put the matter . . . in such a form, and if I have done so it has been an inadvertence, and indeed I did not mean to complain, but rather to explain the reason of , . . the noise."

"Please tell me whatever you please, but it was not noise, for I heard some words. . . ."

"The rivers of Damascus? I feared so, sir; that was the climax or point of repetition—but I will relate the matter in order, with your permission.

"It has been my habit, after I have duly examined a passage in the original language and the light of competent scholars, and verified its lessons by my own reason and conscience—collected the raw material, if I may so say—to commit the same to writing according to my ability, using language that can be understood of the people, and yet conforming as far as may be to the Elizabethan standard."

In my opinion, I indicated, he had done well.

"I judged that I would have your approval so far, but hereafter comes in a grave question of expediency, on which I should like your mind as a neutral person and one given to literary pursuits. My habit is farther to read to the people what I have written in a clear voice, and with such animation as is natural to me, in the faith that whatsoever may have been given me by the Spirit of Truth may be witnessed to the hearers by the same Spirit."

This appeared to me a very reasonable method and a just hope.

"Others, however, acting according to their nature, commit their message to memory, and deliver it to the people with many lively and engaging

A PROBATIONER

gestures, which pleases the people and wins their hearts."

"And so the groundlings prefer the wind-bags," I interrupted, "and elect them to be their minister."

"It is not so that I wished you to infer," and the probationer's voice was full of reproof, "for I trust my desire is not to obtain a church, but the confirmation of my calling through the voice of the people; yet who knoweth his heart?" And the probationer was much distressed.

It was only my foolish thought, I hastened to explain, and besought him to continue.

"A friend of . . . much shrewdness and, I am sure, of good intention, has spoken to me at length on my . . . want of favour with the people, and has pointed out that the Word must be placed before them after a winsome fashion."

"And so?"

"He urged me to choose texts which could be frequently repeated with effect, and so lodge their idea in the mind of the people, and that I should not use any manuscript, but should employ certain arts of oratory, such as beginning low and raising the voice up to a climax where it would be good to repeat the text with emphasis.

"As an example and . . . inducement he dwelt upon the case of one probationer who had taken for his text, 'And there shall be no more sea,' whereon he composed a single sermon, to which he devoted much pains. This he delivered daily for some hours in his chamber, and at the end of each paragraph said in a loud voice, 'And there shall be no more sea.' He was elected to three churches within a short space," concluded Mr. Clunas.

"You have therefore thought it desirable to amend your habit."

"Well, so far," and the probationer was much embarrassed, "it was impossible for me to handle what my adviser called 'repeaters,' such as that I have mentioned, for my mind does not incline to them; but as I had been labouring the tendency to prefer meretricious and sensational religion to that which is austere and pure from the text, 'Are not Abana and Pharpar, rivers of Damascus, better than all the waters of Israel?' it seemed to me that I might for once . . . make trial . . . that is, use the words Abana and Pharpar as a symbol to . . . fix the truth, as it were. It is very laborious and . . . not grateful to me. Do you think that . . . I am doing right?" and my probationer fixed me with an anxious eye.

"Quite so, sir, I understand perfectly," as I was making a blundering effort to suggest that Providence hardly intended that my probationer should go round the country like a showman with "repeaters." "You have confirmed my own idea and . . . delivered my feet from falling, for I had come nearly to unreality in a holy thing, besides ridding me from an irksome task," and he regarded the sheets—the "rivers" standing out in half text—with strong dislike.

"There is another matter," he continued, "on which I would fain have your mind, since you have shown so much sympathy. It is now, I regret to say, the custom for a person in my position, that is, on probation, to print a number of certificates from influential persons and send them to . . . the authorities in a vacant church. This I have refused to do; but there is a special reason why I strongly desire to be settled . . . not quite unworthy, I hope," and a faint flush came to the probationer's face.

"I understand"—for it was natural to suppose that he was engaged, as many in his circumstances are, which grows into a pathetic tragedy as a girl waits for long years till her betrothed is approved in his work and can offer her a home—"and you have got your certificates."

"A few, and it may be that I could secure more; here is one which . . . I value deeply . . . count above gold. It's from Prof. Carphin; you know what he has done, of course.

"Hebrew scholar"—the probationer rose from his chair and paced the floor—"that is inadequate, quite inadequate; there are many Hebrew scholars, thank God, but Prof. Carphin has gone deeper. Why, sir, he has made a race of scholars, and changed the face of theological thought in Scotland; he is the modern Erasmus of our land," and the probationer was very warm.

"This is what he has written of me, and it is superfluous to say that from such a man this testimony is the highest praise; I ought hardly to show such words, but you will not misjudge me."

"I beg to certify that Mr. Hiram Clunas, Master of Arts and Bachelor of Divinity, late Fellow of this College, is in my judgment fully competent to expound the Hebrew Scriptures after an accurate and spiritual fashion to any body of intelligent people.
"ZECHARIAH CARPHIN,
"D.D., LL.D.
"CALVIN COLLEGE, EDINBURGH."

"Pardon me, it is my foolishness, but you notice 'fully'; this extremity of language is, I need not say, undeserved, but that Dr. Carphin should have written it is . . . a compensation for many little disappointments," and the probationer's voice trembled.

"No, it will not be of material service in the way of gaining me a hearing, for it is a . . . moral disgrace to my Church that the word of this eminent man carries little weight with . . . committees and such like, and that many people in this University city do not know his face when he walks along Princes Street.

A PROBATIONER

"This is from another kind of man, who is very . . . acceptable as a preacher, and has much influence . . . in vacancies; it was an indiscretion, I fear, to have asked him for . . . a certificate, as he has only seen me once; but when one is pressed he is not always wise."

"I have had the pleasure of knowing the Rev. Hiram Clunas for a considerable time, and have much satisfaction in recommending him to the favourable consideration of selection committees of vacant congregations. He is a ripe scholar, a profound divine, an eloquent preacher, a faithful pastor, an experienced Christian, with an attractive and popular manner, and general knowledge of a varied and rich character. Any congregation securing Mr. Clunas is certain to increase both in number and finance, and I anticipate for this talented young minister a future of remarkable and rapid success.
"MacDuff MacLeear, D.D."

"Yes, it is a curious name, and I believe was, so to say adopted. Originally he was James MacLeear—MacLeear is his own—and some years ago he inserted MacDuff, I am credibly informed, and now he has dropped his Christian name.
"The reason for the change, it is understood, is for purposes of advertisement in the public prints, where, I am informed, ordinary names such as

James or John are less . . . striking, so that preachers who desire to appeal to the people use two surnames, as it were; it seems to me doubtful in ethics, but one must not be ready to judge his neighbour in such straits.

"No, his degree is not from a Scots University, but from a seat of learning in a Western State of America—Auroraville, I think it is called, but I am not sure. Yes, he wrote a little book on the *Maidens of the Bible* of a popular cast.

"You agree with me that no one could use such a testimony with . . . self-respect, and I have resolved to print no certificates or make any personal appeal; but I do not regret the effort I made, for it has gained me the Professor's letter," and the probationer folded up the letter carefully and placed it in his desk.

"I fear that you must think me charged with vain ambition, but . . . it is not for my own sake."

From time to time we spent an hour together, and he told me of his journeys, many and toilsome.

"Of course I am not sent to supply in cities, for they require men of greater . . . experience; my allotment is always in the country, and I like that better.

"When my station comes near I begin to look out of the window and see whether the district is level or hilly—for though climbing tries one a little, one has a fair view to refresh the soul, and I like

A PROBATIONER

woods because of the mystery and the rustling of the leaves.

"Sometimes a farmer will meet me with a dogcart—and there are no men so kind as farmers—but mostly I walk, and that is nothing unless the distance be far and it be raining heavily. No, it may be a weakness of the flesh, but I do not like a night walk, and yet to see the squares of light in the cottage windows, flashing across a glen or breaking out of a wood, is very pleasing."

One snowy morning in February he came into my room in evident excitement, with a letter in his hand.

"You have taken such an interest in my affairs that I thought you would like to know . . . I have received a letter informing me that I am on the short leet for Tilliegask . . . just two, and I am one . . . and I am to preach next Sabbath . . . and the farmer with whom I stayed has sent a very encouraging letter."

During the week the probationer was much tried on a question of conscience, whether he ought to act on a suggestion of his friend at Tilliegask.

"It happens," he explained to me, "that the people at Tilliegask are very conservative in their views of the Bible, while, as you are aware, I have been led to accept certain modern conclusions regarding the history of the books, and my good friend desires that I should . . . make no allusion to them in my discourse.

"Now," went on the probationer, "it was not my intention to do so, but after this advice am I not bound in conscience to indicate, simply to indicate, my position, that they may not be deceived, and that I may not obtain a church by guile?" And he read to me the sentence, which I make no doubt no one understood, but which was to Mr. Clunas a great relief. He came home from Tilliegask in high spirits, and speculated every evening on his chances as against the other man who was to preach on Sabbath.

"No, he was not what you would call a scholar," and then the probationer laughed aloud—a rare occurrence; "well it was a translation in the Latin class; he rendered *adhuc juvenis* as 'a still youth,' which was much tasted, and others, too, as remarkable; but it is not generous to remember such . . . failings."

The good man was indeed so distressed by this disparaging allusion to his rival that he searched his heart for the sins of pride and jealousy, which with envy and worldliness, he confessed to me, constantly beset him. He also impressed upon me that although Mr. Tosh might not be a scholar in the academic sense, yet he had such gifts of speech that he would be an excellent minister for Tilliegask if the choice of that secluded place should fall on Tosh. But the probationer waited anxiously for the first post on Tuesday, which would give the result, and I was only less anxious.

When he did not come down with tidings, and only the faintest sound came from his room as of a chair occasionally shifted before the fire, I went up, and found my friend very low and two open letters on the table.

"It has not been . . . God's will," and he signed that I should read the letters. One was from the ecclesiastical functionary who presides over elections and church courts, and who is called by the suggestive name of "moderator"; that the vote had been fifty-two for Mr. Clunas and ninety-three for Mr. Tosh; that Mr. Tosh had been elected; that on his, the moderator's appeal, the minority had "fallen in;" that he, the moderator, was sure that Mr. Clunas would be pleased to know that his supporters had shown so good a spirit, and that there was no doubt that the Great Head of the Church had something in store for His servant; and that in the event of Mr. Clunas applying in another vacancy he, the moderator, would be willing to give him a strong certificate as to the impression he, Mr. Clunas, had produced on the congregation of Tilliegask. The second letter was from Wester Tilliegask, my friend's host, who was full of genuine regret that Mr. Clunas had not won the poll, who explained that up to Sabbath his chance was excellent, but that Mr. Tosh had carried all before him by a sermon on "A Rainbow round about the Throne," with very fetching illustrations and quotations—Mr. Tosh had also won several votes by shaking hands with the people at the door, and ingeniously giving it to be understood that his idea of pastoral duty was to visit his congregation four times a year; that, notwithstanding all these Tosh attractions, he, Wester Tilliegask, would have preferred Mr. Clunas; and that as there was a rumour that the minister of Ballengeich would soon need a colleague, he would arrange through his, Wester Tilliegask's, wife's brother that Mr. Clunas should have a hearing. He added that a certificate from MacDuff MacLeear, placing Mr. Tosh a little lower than St. Paul, had told.

The probationer was very brave and generous, blaming no one, and acknowledging that Tosh would be a more suitable man for Tilliegask, but it was evident he was hardly hit.

"It was not to escape the unrest of this life," he said, "nor for the position, nor even for the sanction of my work; it was for the sake of one who . . . has waited long to see me an ordained minister. She may not . . . be spared much longer; my mother is now nearly seventy." So it was no sweetheart, but his mother of whom he thought.

"If I had been elected, I had purposed to start this forenoon and carry the news myself, and I imagined the scene. I never could reach the cottage unseen, for there is a window in the gable which commands the road, so that mother is ever waiting at the garden gate for me.

"Do not count me foolish, but I was to pretend that I had just come to visit her for a day, and then ask her how she would like to leave the cottage and live in a manse.

"By this time she would jalouse something—'tis her word—but I would tell nothing, only expatiate on the manse and her room in it, and . . . and . . . she would suddenly throw her arms round my neck. . . . Excuse me, sir; I will come down in the evening, if you please."

Before evening he was hurrying down to the cottage, for after all he had to go to his mother, and when he came back next Monday she was dead and buried.

"Your sympathy is very grateful," as we sat together, "and it helps me, but I think my heart is . . . broken; although I had to live in Edinburgh in order to accomplish my railway journeys, and we only saw one another at intervals, we were all in all to one another. . . .

"There were things passed between us I cannot tell, for it seems to me that a mother's death-bed is a holy place; but she knew that I had lost Tilliegask, and . . . she was not cast down, as I was for her sake.

"'Dinna lose heart, Hiram,' she said, her hand in mine, 'for my faith will be justified; when I gave ye to the Lord the day your father died I was sure, a' through the fecht o' education I was sure, an' when you got your honours I was sure, an' when you got no kirk I was still as sure, and now my eyes are clear, an' I see that God has savit you for a work that hath not entered into my heart,' and she blessed me. . . ."

From that day he began to fail, and although he struggled to fulfil preaching engagements, he had at last to give up public work. But he toiled harder than ever at the Semitic languages.

"It is not that I am deceiving myself with vain hopes," he explained to me one day, "for I know full well that I am dying, but it seemeth good that whatsoever talent I have should be cultivated to the end.

"The future life is veiled, and speculation is vain, but language must be used, and they who have mastered the ancient roots will be of some service; it is all I can offer, and I must give of my best."

The morning he died I looked over his few affairs and balanced his accounts, which were kept in a small pass-book, his poor fees on one side and his slender expenses on the other to a halfpenny.

"The expenditure may seem heavy the last few journeys, but my strength failed by the way, and I was unable to walk to my destination, but there may still be enough at the end of the week for what has to be done.

"There will be £9 15s. 6d. when all is paid.

"With the sale of my books it will suffice, for I have carefully enquired, to buy a grave and defray the cost of burial. It is not possible to be buried beside my mother, for our ground is full, so let me lie where the sun is shining on the Grange Cemetery."

Soon after his mind wandered, and I gathered he was in the vestry of Tilliegask Kirk.

"Lord be merciful to me and remember my infirmities . . . deliver Thy servant from the fear of man and all doubleness of heart . . . give me grace to declare Thy truth and to set Thee before me . . . bless my mother and hear her prayers. . . ."

After a little while he began to preach, but we could make nothing of the words till he suddenly stopped and raised himself in the bed.

"Thou, Lord," he cried, with great astonishment, "hearing me . . . Forgive . . . I am not worthy to declare Thy Gospel. . . ."

What was said by the Master none of us heard, but the astonishment passed into joy, and the light thereof still touched and made beautiful his face as the probationer fell on sleep.

It was a spring day when we laid his body to rest, and any one who cares can find his grave, because a weeping willow hangs over it, and this is the inscription on the stone:

HIRAM CLUNAS,

Probationer.

"It is a very small thing that I should be judged of man's judgment."

A GOVERNMENT OFFICIAL

A GOVERNMENT OFFICIAL

Never had I met any man so methodical in his habits, so neat in his dress, so accurate in speech, so precise in manner as my fellow-lodger. When he took his bath in the morning I knew it was half-past seven, and when he rang for hot water that it was a quarter to eight. Until a quarter-past he moved about the room in his slow, careful dressing, and then everything was quiet next door till half-past eight, when the low murmur of the Lord's Prayer concluded his devotions. Two minutes later he went downstairs—if he met a servant one could hear him say " Good morning " —and read his newspaper—he seldom had letters— till nine, when he rang for breakfast. Twenty-past nine he went upstairs and changed his coat, and he spent five minutes in the lobby selecting a pair of gloves, brushing his hat, and making a last survey for a speck of dust. One glove he put on opposite the hat-stand, and the second on the doorstep, and when he touched the pavement you might have set your watch by nine-thirty. Once he was in the lobby at five and twenty minutes to ten, distressed and flurried.

138 A GOVERNMENT OFFICIAL

"I cut my chin slightly when shaving," he explained, "and the wound persists in bleeding. It has an untidy appearance, and a drop of blood might fall on a letter."

The walk that morning was quite broken, and before reaching the corner, he had twice examined his chin with a handkerchief, and shaken his head as one whose position in life was now uncertain.

"It is nothing in itself," he said afterwards, with an apologetic allusion to his anxiety, "and might not matter to another man. But any little misadventure—a yesterday's collar or a razor cut, or even an inky finger—would render me helpless in dealing with people. They would simply look at the weak spot, and one would lose all authority. Some of the juniors smile when I impress on them to be very careful about their dress—quiet, of course, as becomes their situation, but unobjectionable. With more responsibility they will see the necessity of such details. I will remember your transparent sticking-plaster—a most valuable suggestion."

His name was Frederick Augustus Perkins; so ran the card he left on my table a week after I settled in the next rooms, and the problem of his calling gradually became a standing vexation. It fell under the class of conundrums, and one remembered from childhood that it is mean to be told the answer, so I could not say to Mister Perkins—for it was characteristic of the prim little man that no properly constituted person could have said Perkins—

"By the way, what is your line of things?" or any more decorous rendering of my curiosity.

Mrs. Holmes, who was as a mother to Mr. Perkins and myself, as well as two younger men of literary pursuits and irregular habits, had a gift of charming irrelevance, and was able to combine allusions to Mr. Perkins' orderly life and the amatory tendencies of a new cook in a mosaic of enthralling interest.

"No, Betsy Jane has 'ad her notice and goes this day week; not that her cookin's bad, but her brothers don't know when to leave. One was 'ere no later than last night, though if he was her born brother, 'e 'ad a different father and mother, or my name ain't 'Olmes. 'Your brother, Betsy Jane,' says I, 'ought not to talk in a strange 'ouse on family affairs till eleven o'clock.'

"''E left at 'alf-past ten, punctual,' says she, looking as hinnocent as a child, 'for I 'eard Mr. Perkins go up to 'is room as I was lettin' Jim out.'

"'Betsy Jane,' I says, quite calm, 'where do you expeck to go to as doesn't know wot truth is?' for Mr. Perkins leaves 'is room has the 'all clock starts on eleven, and 'e's in 'is bedroom at the last stroke. If she 'adn't brought in Mr. Perkins she might 'ave deceived me, gettin' old and not bein' so quick in my hearing as I was; but that settled her.

"'Alf-past,'" went on Mrs. Holmes, scornfully;

"and 'im never varied two minutes the last ten years, except one night 'e fell asleep in 'is chair, being bad with hinfluenza.

"For a regular single gentleman as rises in the morning and goes out, and comes in and takes 'is dinner, and goes to bed like the Medes and Persians, I've never seen 'is equal; an' it's five-and-twenty-years since 'Olmes died, 'avin' a bad liver through takin' gin for rheumatics; an' Lizbeth Peevey says to me, 'Take lodgers, Jemima; not that they pays for the trouble, but it 'ill keep an 'ouse.' . . .

"Mr. Perkins' business;" it was shabby, but the temptation came as a way of escape from the flow of Mrs. Holmes' autobiography; "now that I couldn't put a name on, for why, 'e never speaks about 'is affairs; just 'Good evening, Mrs. 'Olmes; I'll take fish for breakfast to-morrow;' no more than that, or another blanket on 'is bed on the first of November, for it's by days, not cold, 'e goes. . . ."

It was evident that I must solve the problem for myself.

Mr. Perkins could not be a city man, for in the hottest June he never wore a white waistcoat, nor had he the swelling gait of one who made an occasional *coup* in mines, and it went without saying that he did not write; a man who went to bed at eleven, and whose hair made no claim to distinction. One's mind fell back on the idea of law—

A GOVERNMENT OFFICIAL

conveyancing seemed probable—but his face lacked sharpness, and the alternative of confidential clerk to a firm of drysalters was contradicted by an air of authority that raised observations on the weather to the level of a state document. The truth came upon me—a flash of inspiration—as I saw Mr. Perkins coming home one evening. The black frock coat and waistcoat, dark grey trousers, spotless linen, high, old-fashioned collar, and stiff stock, were a symbol, and could only mean one profession.

"By the way, Mr. Perkins," for this was all one now required to know, "are you Income Tax or Stamps?"

"Neither, although my duty makes me familiar with every department in the Civil Service. I have the honour to be," and he cleared his throat with dignity, "a first-class clerk in the Schedule Office.

"Our work," he explained to me, "is very important, and in fact . . . vital to the administration of affairs. The efficiency of practical government depends on the accuracy of the forms issued, and every one is composed in our office.

"No, that is a common mistake," in reply to my shallow remark; "the departments do not draw up their own forms, and in fact they are not fit for such work. They send us a memorandum of what their officials wish to ask, and we put it into shape.

"It requires long experience and, I may say, some . . . ability to compose a really creditable schedule, one that will bring out every point clearly and exhaustively—in fact, I have ventured to call it a science "—here Mr. Perkins allowed himself to smile—" and it might be defined Schedulology.

"Yes, to see a double sheet of foolscap divided up into some twenty-four compartments, each with a question and a blank space for the answer is pleasing to the eye, very pleasing indeed.

"What annoys one," and Mr. Perkins became quite irritable, " is to examine a schedule after it has been filled and to discover how it has been misused—simply mangled.

"It is not the public simply who are to blame; they are, of course, quite hopeless, and have an insane desire to write their names all over the paper, with family details; but members of the Civil Service abuse the most admirable forms that ever came out of our office.

"Numerous? Yes, naturally so; and as governmental machinery turns on schedules they will increase every year. Could you guess, now, the number of different schedules under our charge?"

"Several hundred, perhaps."

Mr. Perkins smiled with much complacency. "Sixteen thousand four hundred and four, besides temporary ones that are only used in emergencies. One department has now reached twelve hundred and two; it has been admirably organised, and its secretary could tell you the subject of every form.

"Well, it does not become me to boast, but I

have had the honour of contributing two hundred and twenty myself, and have composed forty-two more that have not yet been accepted.

"Well, yes," he admitted, with much modesty, "I have kept copies of the original drafts," and he showed me a bound volume of his works.

"An author? It is very good of you to say so," and Mr. Perkins seemed much pleased with the idea, twice smiling to himself during the evening, and saying as we parted, "It's my good fortune to have a large and permanent circulation."

All November Mr. Perkins was engaged with what he hoped would be one of his greatest successes.

"It's a sanitation schedule for the Education Department, and is, I dare to say, nearly perfect. It has eighty-three questions on every point, from temperature to drains, and will present a complete view of the physical condition of primary schools.

"You have no idea," he continued, "what a fight I have had with our Head to get it through—eight drafts, each one costing three days' labour—but now he has passed it.

"'Perkins,' he said, 'this is the most exhaustive schedule you have ever drawn up, and I'm proud it's come through the hands of the drafting sub-department. Whether I can approve it as Head of the publishing sub-department is very doubtful.'"

"Do you mean that the same man would approve your paper in one department to-day and . . ."

"Quite so. It's a little difficult for an outsider to appreciate the perfect order—perhaps I might say symmetry—of the Civil Service," and Mr. Perkins spoke with a tone of condescension as to a little child. "The Head goes himself to the one sub-department in the morning and to the other in the afternoon, and he acts with absolute impartiality.

"Why, sir,"—Mr. Perkins began to warm and grow enthusiastic,—"I have received a letter from the other sub-department, severely criticising a draft he had highly commended in ours two days before, and I saw his hand in the letter . . . distinctly; an able review, too, very able indeed.

"'Very well put, Perkins,' he said to me himself; 'they've found the weak points; we must send an amended draft;' and so we did, and got a very satisfactory reply. It was a schedule about swine fever, 972 in the department of Agriculture. I have had the pleasure of reading it in public circulation when on my holidays."

"Does your Head sign the letters addressed to himself?"

"Certainly; letters between departments are always signed by the chief officer." Mr. Perkins seemed to have found another illustration of public ignorance, and recognised his duty as a missionary of officialism. "It would afford me much pleasure to give you any information regarding our excellent system, which has been slowly built up and will repay study; but you will excuse me this evening, as I am indisposed—a tendency to shiver which annoyed me in the office to-day."

Next morning I rose half an hour late, as Mr. Perkins did not take his bath, and was not surprised when Mrs. Holmes came to my room, overflowing with concern and disconnected speech.

" 'E's that regular in 'is ways, that when 'Annah Mariar says 'is water's at 'is door at eight o'clock, I went up that 'urried that I couldn't speak; and I 'ears him speaking to 'isself, which is not what you would expect of him, he being the quietest gentleman as ever . . ."

"Is Mr. Perkins ill, do you mean?" for Mrs. Holmes seemed now in fair breath, and was always given to comparative reviews.

" So I knocks and says, ' Mr. Perkins, 'ow are you feeling?' and all I could 'ear was 'temperance'; it's little as he needs of that, for excepting a glass of wine at his dinner, and it might be something 'ot before going to bed in winter. . . .

" So I goes in," resumed Mrs. Holmes, "an' there 'e was sittin' up in 'is bed, with 'is face as red as fire, an' not knowing me from Adam. If it wasn't for 'is 'abits an' a-catching of 'is breath you wud 'ave said drink, for 'e says, ' How often have the drains been sluiced last year?'" After which I went up to Mr. Perkins' room without ceremony.

He was explaining, with much cogency, as it seemed to me, that unless the statistics of tempera-

146 A GOVERNMENT OFFICIAL

ture embraced the whole year, they would afford no reliable conclusions regarding the sanitary condition of Board Schools; but when I addressed him by name with emphasis, he came to himself with a start.

"Excuse me, sir; I must apologise . . . I really did not hear . . . in fact," and then, as he realised his situation, Mr. Perkins was greatly embarrassed.

"Did I forget myself so far as . . . to send for you? . . . I was not feeling well. I have a slight difficulty in breathing, but I am quite able to go to the office . . . in a cab.

"You are most kind and obliging, but the schedule I am . . . it just comes and goes . . . thank you, no more water . . . is important and . . . intricate; no one . . . can complete it . . . except myself.

"With your permission I will rise . . . in a few minutes . . . ten o'clock, dear me . . . this is most unfortunate . . . not get down till eleven . . . I must really insist . . ." But the doctor had come, and Mr. Perkins obeyed on one condition.

"Yes, doctor, I prefer, if you please, to know; you see I am not a young person . . . nor nervous . . . thank you very much . . . quite so; pneumonia is serious . . . and double pneumonia dangerous, I understand . . . no, it is not that . . . one is not alarmed at my

A GOVERNMENT OFFICIAL

age, but . . . yes, I'll lie down . . . letter must go to office . . . dictate it to my friend . . . certain form . . . leave of absence, in fact . . . trouble you too much . . . medical certificate."

He was greatly relieved after this letter was sent by special messenger with the key of his desk, and quite refreshed when a clerk came up with the chief's condolences.

" My compliments to Mr. Lighthead . . . an excellent young official, very promising indeed . . . and would he step upstairs for a minute . . . will excuse this undress in circumstances . . . really I will not speak any more.

" Those notes, Mr. Lighthead, will make my idea quite plain . . . and I hope to revise final draft . . . if God will . . . my dutiful respect to the Board, and kind regards to the chief clerk . . . it was kind of you to come, most thoughtful."

This young gentleman came into my room to learn the state of the case, and was much impressed.

" Really this kind of thing—Perkins gasping in bed and talking in his old-fashioned way—knocks one out of time, don't you know? If he had gone on much longer I should have bolted.

" Like him in the office? I should think so. You should have seen the young fellows to-day when they heard he was so ill. Of course we laugh a bit at him—Schedule Perkins he's called—because he's so dry and formal; but that's nothing.

"With all his little cranks, he knows his business better than any man in the department; and then he's a gentleman, d'y see? could not say a rude word or do a mean thing to save his life—not made that way, in fact.

"Let me just give you one instance—show you his sort. Every one knew that he ought to have been chief clerk, and that Rodway's appointment was sheer influence. The staff was mad, and some one said Rodway need not expect to have a particularly good time.

"Perkins overheard him, and chipped in at once. 'Mr. Rodway'—you know his dry manner, wagging his eyeglass all the time—' is our superior officer, and we are bound to render him every assistance in our power, or,' and then he was splendid, 'resign our commissions.' Rodway, they say, has retired; but the worst of it is that as Perkins has been once passed over he 'ill not succeed.

"Perhaps it won't matter, poor chap. I say," said Lighthead, hurriedly, turning his back and examining a pipe on the mantel-piece, "do you think he is going to . . . I mean, has he a chance?"

"Just a chance, I believe. Have you been long with him?"

"That's not it—it's what he's done for a . . . for fellows. Strangers don't know Perkins. You

A GOVERNMENT OFFICIAL 149

might talk to him for a year, and never hear anything but shop. Then one day you get into a hole, and you would find out another Perkins.

"Stand by you?" and he wheeled round. "Rather, and no palaver either: with money and with time and with . . . other things that do a fellow more good than the whole concern, and no airs. There's more than one man in our office has cause to . . . bless Schedule Perkins.

"Let me tell you how he got . . . one chap out of the biggest scrape he'll ever fall into. Do you mind me smoking?" And then he made himself busy with matches and a pipe that was ever going out for the rest of the story.

"Well, you see, this man, clerk in our office, had not been long up from the country, and he was young. Wasn't quite bad, but he couldn't hold his own with older fellows.

"He got among a set that had suppers in their rooms, and gambled a bit, and he lost and borrowed, and . . . in fact, was stone broke.

"It's not very pleasant for a fellow to sit in his room a week before Christmas, and know that he may be cashiered before the holidays, and all through his own fault.

"If it were only himself, why, he might take his licking and go to the Colonies; but it was hard . . . on his mother—it's always going out, this pipe—when he was her only son, and she rather . . . believed in him.

"Didn't sleep much that night—told me himself afterwards—and he concluded that the best way out was to buy opium in the City next day, and take it—pretty stiff dose, you know—next night.

"Cowardly rather, of course, but it might be easier for the mater down in Devon—his mother, I mean—did I say he was Devon?—same county as myself—affair would be hushed up, and she would have . . . his memory clean.

"As it happened, though, he didn't buy any opium next day—didn't get the chance; for Perkins came round to his desk, and asked this young chap to have a bit of dinner with him—aye, and made him come.

"He had the jolliest little dinner ready you ever saw, and he insisted on the fellow smoking, though Perkins hates the very smell of 'baccy, and—well, he got the whole trouble out of him, except the opium.

"D'y think he lectured and scolded? Not a bit—that's not Perkins—he left the fool to do his own lecturing, and he did it stiff. I'll tell you what he said: 'Your health must have been much tried by this anxiety, so you must go down and spend Christmas with your mother, and I would venture to suggest that you take her a suitable gift.

"'With regard to your debt, you will allow me,' and Perkins spoke as if he had been explaining a schedule, 'to take it over, on two conditions—that

A GOVERNMENT OFFICIAL 151

you repay me by instalments every quarter, and dine with me every Saturday evening for six months.'

"See what he was after? Wanted to keep . . . the fellow straight, and cheer him up; and you've no idea how Perkins came out those Saturdays—capital stories as ever you heard—and he declared that it was a pleasure to him.

"'I am rather lonely,' he used to say, 'and it is most kind of a young man to sit with me.' Kind!"

"What was the upshot with your friend? Did he turn over a new leaf?"

"He 'ill never be the man that Perkins expects, but he's doing his level best, and . . . is rising in the office. Perkins swears by him, and that's made a man of the fellow.

"He's paid up the cash now, but . . . he can never pay up the kindness—confound those wax matches, they never strike—he told his mother last summer the whole story.

"She wrote to Perkins—of course I don't know what was in the letter—but Perkins had the fellow into his room. 'You ought to have regarded our transaction as confidential. I am grieved you mentioned my name;' and then as I—I mean, as the fellow—was going out, 'I'll keep that letter beside my commission,' said Perkins.

"If Perkins dies"—young men don't do that kind of thing, or else one would have thought— "it 'ill be . . . a beastly shame," which was a terrible collapse, and Mr. Geoffrey Lighthead, of the Schedule Department, left the house without further remark or even shaking hands.

That was Wednesday, and on Friday morning he appeared, flourishing a large blue envelope sealed with an imposing device, marked "On Her Majesty's Service," and addressed to—

"Frederick Augustus Perkins, Esq.,
"First Class Clerk in the Schedule Department,
"Somerset House,
"London,"

an envelope any man might be proud to receive, and try to live up to for a week.

"Rodway has retired," he shouted, "and we can't be sure in the office, but the betting is four to one—I'm ten myself—that the Board has appointed Perkins Chief Clerk," and Lighthead did some steps of a triumphal character.

"The Secretary appeared this morning after the Board had met. 'There's a letter their Honours wish taken at once to Mr. Perkins. Can any of you deliver it as his residence?' Then the other men looked at me, because—well, Perkins has been friendly with me; and that hansom came very creditably indeed.

"Very low, eh? Doctors afraid not last over the night—that's hard lines . . . but I say, they did not reckon on this letter. Could not you read it to him? You see this was his one ambition. He could never be Secretary, not able enough, but he was made for Chief Clerk. Now he's got it, or I would not have been sent out skimming with this letter. Read it to him, and the dear old chap will be on his legs in a week."

It seemed good advice, and this was what I read, while Perkins lay very still and did his best to breathe:—

"DEAR MR. PERKINS,—

"I have the pleasure to inform you that the Board have appointed you Chief Clerk in the Schedule Department in succession to Gustavus Rodway, Esq., who retires, and their Honours desire me further to express their appreciation of your long and valuable service, and their earnest hope that you may be speedily restored to health. I am,
"Your obedient servant,
"ARTHUR WRAXHALL,
"*Secretary.*"

For a little time it was too much for Mr. Perkins, and then he whispered:—

"The one thing on earth I wished, and . . . more than I deserved . . . not usual, personal references in Board letters . . . perhaps hardly regular . . . but most gratifying . . . and . . . strengthening.

"I feel better already . . . some words I would like to hear again . . . thank you, where I can reach it . . . ., nurse will be so good as to read it.".

Mr. Perkins revived from that hour, having his tonic administered at intervals, and astonished the doctors. On Christmas Eve he had made such progress that Lighthead was allowed to see him for five minutes.

"Heard about your calling three times a day . . . far too kind with all your work . . . and the messages from the staff . . . touched me to heart . . . never thought had so many friends . . . wished been more friendly myself.

"My promotion, too . . . hope may be fit for duty . . . can't speak much, but think I'll be spared . . . Almighty very good to me . . . Chief Clerk of Schedule Department . . . would you mind saying Lord's Prayer together . . . it sums up everything."

So we knelt one on each side of Perkins' bed, and I led with "Our Father"—the other two being once or twice quite audible. The choir of a neighbouring church were singing a Christmas carol in the street, and the Christ came into our hearts as a little child.

THE RIGHT HAND OF SAMUEL DODSON

THE RIGHT HAND OF SAMUEL DODSON

I.

"Smoking, as usual, and wasting your time after luncheon, instead of hurrying to your offices and coining time into money like old Sam Dodson, who can give the cash value of every five minutes," and Welsby sat down beside three other young Liverpool merchants in the club—all men who had one eye on business and the other on the good of the city. "Something's happened since I saw you fellows last on 'Change. Guess."

"Cotton up three points? A corn corner at Chicago? A big bear in lard? Anything to do with fruit?"

"Nothing whatever to do with such prosaic subjects, and I am ashamed to notice your mercenary tempers; this is a public affair, and is to be a profound secret for exactly seventy minutes, after which it will appear in the fourth edition of the *Evening Trumpet.*

"It's a pity that the early news could not be used for an operation in cotton, but I'll take it along to the ' Flags,' and tell it under pledge of silence to half a dozen brokers. If you are really interested in the matter, this will give it a wider and more certain circulation than any *Trumpet* could."

"We're all ears, Welsby."

"Well, to begin at the beginning, you know how our people in Liverpool are crowded together in courts and rookeries without room or air. It's hard on the men and women, but it's hardest on the children, who have no place to play in but the gutter.

"So a man wrote a letter to the papers about a month ago, pleading for a fund to put down small playgrounds in the crowded districts, where the little folk could come of an evening, and the mothers could sit, and the men might smoke a pipe. . . ."

"I remember the letter," broke in Cotton; "it was signed 'Philanthropist,' and was generally supposed to have been composed in a moment of inspiration by some proprietor of insanitary property; it was an elegant letter, and affected me very much—to tears, in fact."

"It was signed 'Charles Welsby,' and you never read a word of it, because it had no reference to polo nor the Macfarlane Institute for Working Lads, the only subjects to which you give any attention. Four people read it, however, and wrote to me at once. One man denounced the scheme as another instance of the patronage of the rich. He added that it was a sop, and that the toilers would soon find open places for themselves."

"He would mean your garden, Welsby," suggested Lard. "The Socialist has two main principles of action: first, to give nothing to any good cause himself; and second, to appropriate his neighbour's property on the first opportunity. And your other correspondents?"

"I had a letter from the inventor of a non-intoxicating beer, offering £5 on condition that we advertised his beverage, which he discovered by supernatural guidance and sold for philanthropic ends."

"All queer beverages and patent medicines are owned by high-class religious people, as far as I can understand," remarked Corn. "Go on."

"A third letter warned me that such spaces would be abused by bad characters and sap the morals of the people; the writer also wanted to know whether they would be closed on the Sabbath."

"A publican evidently," remarked Cotton; "no man is so concerned about Sabbath observance. And so you got sick of the whole affair?"

"Rather, till I got this letter. I'll read it, and then you can make your guesses at the enclosure.

"'LIVERPOOL, *June* 9, 189-.

"'MY DEAR SIR,—Your letter of 7th ult., in the issue of the *Morning Trumpet* of May 8, caught my eye and received my most careful attention. As you appeared to have established a *primâ facie* case for what you designate "People's Playgrounds," I have occupied my leisure time in examining the sanitary and social condition of certain parts of our city which were more or less distinctly indicated in your letter. As the result of my investigations, I am thoroughly convinced, in the first place, that you have proved your case as regards the unfortunate circumstances of the children in such parts, and, in the second place, that your plan for their relief is practical and wisely considered.

"'It then became my duty as a citizen of Liverpool to consider what I could do to further the ends of your scheme, and it seemed to me on the whole most advisable to place a sum of money at your disposal, on condition that it be spent with such other sums as may be sent you in purchasing decaying property and creating playgrounds—said playgrounds to be vested in the Parks and Gardens Committee of the City Council—and I would suggest that people interested in each district be allowed and encouraged to contribute to the furnishing and adornment of the playgrounds.

"'I beg therefore to enclose a draft in your favour on Messrs. Goldbeater & Co., Lombard Street, London, and I have only to add my sincere approval of the good work you are doing among the poor of Liverpool, and my wish, which, as a man of honour, you will doubtless carefully respect, that you will take no steps to discover my name.—I have the honour to be, your obedient servant,

"'ZACCHEUS.'"

"Satisfactory, very, although a trifle pedantic and long-winded. And the sum, Welsby? I say £250."

"£500," said Cotton.

"£1,000," cried Lard.

"What do you say to £10,000?" and the draft was handed round.

"Congratulate you, old man." Corn shook hands with Welsby, and so did they all, for he had worked hard in many a good cause. "You deserve your luck; think I'll take to writing letters for my pet hospital. Who can he be? Do you suspect any one?"

"Half a dozen, but I'm bound not to inquire; and I rather think that the trail is covered at Goldbeater's beyond finding. But I know who did not give it—Sam Dodson.

"No, of course I did not ask him for help. One does not court refusals; but you know his meddling, ferreting ways. If he didn't stop me in the street and ask fifty questions till I hinted at a subscription, when he was off in a minute."

"Nothing frightens him like a suggestion of that kind. He has raised meanness to the height of genius. They say that he is worth £200,000, but I wouldn't change with him," said Lard, "for a million. When he dies, Dodson will not leave a soul to regret him, and there'll not be six people at his funeral."

"You can't be sure, gentlemen," said a quiet voice behind; "I've overheard you on Dodson, and I hope what you say is not true."

The speaker was one of those rare souls God sends forth at a time to establish our faith in goodness; who are believed in by all parties, and respected by all creeds, and loved by all classes; who sit on all the charitable boards, and help on every good cause, and make peace in quarrels; whom old men consult in their perplexities, and young men turn to in trouble, and people follow with affectionate glances in the street; who never suspect their own excellence, always take the lowest seat, and have to be compelled to accept an honour.

"You have a good word to say for everybody, sir," said Cotton with deep respect; "but have you, even, ever got a penny from Mr. Dodson for a charity?"

"Well, I cannot say that I remember an instance; only I'm sure that he has his own way of doing good. Every one has, unless he be utterly bad; and I'm seventy years old, gentlemen, and I never met that kind yet."

"Greatheart is the only man in Liverpool who would say a word for Dodson," said Lard a minute later, "and in this case his charity has rather overshot the mark; but it does one good to hear the old man. He is a walking Sermon on the Mount, and the best thing about him is that he believes in everybody; the very sight of his white hair makes me a better man."

II

" How tired you must be, Fred, after four hours' begging in offices! I'll bring you a cup of tea in the study at once, and then you are to have a nice little dinner all to yourself.

" Oh, no, I've not been extravagant at all, and I've not taken any money out of our alms-box, and I'm not a wicked parson's wife who gets into debt; but a hamper came from the country, with lots of good things in it, and you will have the chicken; the children and I simply rioted in plenty to-day. Now, I'll not hear a word about your expedition until you have had some food."

" There, I feel a perfect glutton, Ethel. I hope you have sent some of the h-hamper to the sick."

" I've done nothing of the kind; every single bit is to be eaten in this Vicarage of St. Ambrose; you would starve yourself and your family for the parish, and I am sure you are the hardest working man in it. Well, have you got the money to furnish the playground of St. Ambrose's? "

" Do you mean have I come home with £54 in my pocket as the result of one r-raid by a poor, dull, s-stammering parson, who couldn't make an eloquent appeal to save his life? "

"You don't stammer, Fred, and I wish you wouldn't say such things; you may . . . hesitate at a time, and I am sure any one would give you money for a good cause, because you are . . . so sincere and . . ."

"That will do, Ethel; it's a great h-help to an obscure parson in the poorest of parishes to have a wife who believes in him, and makes four hundred pounds out of two."

"And now about the money. Was the asking hard?"

"It might have been, but every one was so j-jolly. The first man I went to was Mr. Welsby, and as soon as I came into his room he cried out, 'Was just thinking of you: I hope you're on the w-warpath for that playground, for I've a five-pound note ready for you.'

"He sent me on to a cotton b-broker, and he thanked me several times for coming on such a good errand, and backed up Welsby with five pounds. Every person had a kind word, and by five o'clock I had . . ."

"The whole sum?"

"With six p-pounds over, which will get a little sheltered seat for old people. How good those city fellows are when they fancy a cause."

"And when they fancy the man who pleads it, Fred. Did you not get one refusal?"

"Well, I was h-hurt by one man, who treated me rather shabbily. He allowed me to explain the

whole scheme—swings, sand-heaps, seats and all—
and he asked me a hundred questions about the
parish and my work, till I think he knew as much
about the place as we do ourselves, and then sent
me off without a penny—said he didn't give to subscriptions on p-principle."

"What a mean, hypocritical wretch!"

"I left rather down, for I had lost h-half an
hour with him, and I was afraid I had offended
him by some remark, but when I met Welsby again
in the street and told him, he declared that I ought
not to have been sent there, because D-Dodson—
that's his name—was the most inquisitive and hardest man on 'Change."

"He can't be a gentleman, at any rate, to question you for mere curiosity; I hope you gave him
something to think over."

"No, I didn't; it's no use, and only frets oneself.
He had a big c-chance and lost it. What do you
say to inviting the subscribers down some evening
when the playground is in full occupation? They
will get full value for their money at the sight
of the girls on the swings, and the boys at ball,
and the b-babies scooping up the sand, and the old
folks sunning themselves on their seats."

"It will be splendid; but, Fred, it goes to my
heart that our own boys can have no holiday, and
when their schoolfellows are away in Wales, will
be sweltering in this close house."

"How much have we in the h-holiday fund?"

"Just two pounds and sixpence. Save as I would, that is all I could manage. . . . If we had not given so much away we might . . ."

"You are just as r-ready to give as I am, my little wife, and none of us regret anything we've done for the poor souls around us; but I'm sorry for the boys. Did you tell them?"

"No, I hadn't the heart, so I played the coward and said you were thinking the matter over, and that you would tell them, perhaps, to-morrow morning."

"Do you know I rather s-suspected this would be the end of it, and I was planning how to make the best of things. I made up a series of cheap trips, personally conducted, to New Brighton, and Cheshire, and Hale; you'll give us our l-lunch, and we'll have a regular picnic. I have some old knick-knacks of my schooldays at Shrewsbury, and I'll offer them as p-prizes for the best account of the day. You'll come with us, too, and we'll have a particularly jolly time.

"Letters? The post is late to-night. That is about the c-contract for swings, and this is a diocesan circular, and there is a new company p-prospectus—rather an irony sending it to me—but here are two unknown hands; let us see the news.

"Now isn't this good? £3 for the playground from a Dissenter who c-complains I didn't call on him, and has a kind word about my hard work, as he calls it; and I've been often annoyed at that man for the things he said on Disestablishment. He may say anything he pleases now on a platform; I know there is a kind heart behind the words.

"Will this be more money for the s-swings? Hurrah! here is an enclosure of some sort. But what is this . . . ?"

"What's wrong, Fred? Is any one dead? Are you ill . . . ?"

"Ethel, you are an excellent m-manager." The Vicar, very white as to his cheeks, and somewhat wet as to his eyes, stood on the hearthrug and waved his wife to a distance. "Be g-good enough to secure a commodious farmhouse in North Wales, somewhere between Bettws-y-Coed and Llanberis, for the month of August—with a little f-fishing attached, if possible.

"Please sit down, Ethel, and don't interrupt. I'm sane, quite sane; much p-playground and domestic affliction have not made me mad. Now, where was I? Yes, and arrange quite a s-series of tours round by Festiniog, and up Snowdon, and down to Llandudno, and another to the Menai Straits. . . .

"You are an extravagant, d-dressy woman, Ethel, so you may get a n-natty walking dress and three blouses, but keep a trifle for f-fishing apparatus and special provisions . . . you are t-throttling me . . . then read it yourself, read it aloud, and . . . I will p-process round the table. I wish the boys had not gone to bed."

THE RIGHT HAND

"LIVERPOOL, *July* 16, 189—.

"REVEREND AND DEAR SIR,—It has come to my knowledge from various quarters that you and your devoted partner in life are doing a most beneficent work, both sacred and secular, in a very necessitous district of our great city, and that you are discharging this duty to your fellow-creatures at severe cost to yourselves and your family.

"My observation of life leads me to believe that none of our citizens live harder lives, or make greater sacrifices, than clergymen of limited means whose sphere of labour lies in poor parishes, and, without being in any sense a good man—for my whole life is a struggle with one besetting sin, which often getteth the victory—I have been filled with respectful admiration, and have wished to assist, after a humble fashion, in this Christian service.

"As you may have some difficulty in securing a suitable holiday for your family through your notorious charity—for such is the report concerning you—I venture with much diffidence to enclose a draft on London, which can be cashed at any bank, for your use, under two conditions, which I must charge you to observe: (1) that the whole sum be employed to the last penny in holiday expenses—including such special outfit as may be judged fit by your wife for you all; and (2) that you make no effort to discover the name of your unworthy friend. The endorsement of this draft will be sufficient acknowledgment.

"Trusting you will all have a health-giving, happy, and long holiday,

"I have the honour to be,
"Your humble servant,
"ZACCHEUS."

"Your voice is a little shaky, Ethel . . . don't wonder . . . such nonsense about me and such c-compliments to you . . . yes, it will be g-glorious, another honeymoon, and those rascals of boys, why won't they. . . . Let us thank God, wife; it came from Him. . . ."

III

"You will be pleased to hear, mater, dear, that corn is up twopence a cental, and that the market is buoyant; that's the good of new blood being brought into corn. I would have been lost in medicine.

"I have been studying the career of a corn prince, and it has five chapters. He begins a poor boy—from the North of Ireland by preference, but that is not necessary—then he attracts his chief's attention, who sends him out to America, where even the Yankees can't hold their own with him, and he becomes manager of his firm. His next move is to start in partnership with some young fellow who has money and no brains; by-and-bye he discovers by instinct that corn is going to rise, so he buys it ahead by the cargo, and piles up a gorgeous sum—say one hundred thousand pounds. Afterwards he buys out Emptyhead, and becomes the chief of a big house with lots of juniors, and he ends by being a Bank director and moving resolutions at the Town Hall.

"Please don't interrupt, mother, for I have not done yet. Long before the Town Hall level this rising corn man has gone up by stages from the street off Princes Road to an avenue near the Park, and then into the Park, and perhaps into the country, whence he appears as High Sheriff.

"One minute more, you impatient mother. A certain person who will pretend to be nearly fifty when the corn man comes into his kingdom, but will remain always at twenty-five exactly, and grow prettier every year, will have a better set of rooms in each new house, and, at last, will have her own carriage, and visit whole streets of poor folk, and have all Liverpool blessing her. This is the complete history of the corn man and his mother, as it will be expounded to after generations of schoolboys by informing and moral philanthropists. What do you think of it?"

"I think that you are a brave boy, Jack, and your mother is proud of you and grateful; if it's any reward for you to know this, I can say that the way you have taken your disappointment has been one of my chief comforts in our great sorrow."

"Don't talk as if I were a sort of little tin hero, mater, or else I'll have to leave the room, for I'm nothing of the sort, really. If you only saw me at my desk, or fussing round the offices, or passing the time of day on corn, you would see that I was simply born for business."

"Jack," said Mrs. Laycock solemnly, "you have not been without faults, I'm thankful to say, for you've been hot-tempered, hot-headed, wilful, and lots of things, but this is the first time you have been deliberately untruthful."

"Mother, with all respect to you, I will not stand this insult," and so he slipped down on the floor and caressed his mother's hand. "You think that I've no commercial ability. Wait for the event. It will be swagger, you bet."

"I think everything that is good of you, Jack, as I ought, and your father did; but I know that it was very hard that you could not go back to Rugby this autumn and finish in the sixth, and go to Cambridge and study at Caius, your father's college, and get your M.D., and take up your father's profession and the one you loved, the noblest a man can live and . . . die in," and there was a break in the widow's voice.

"Of course, mater, that is what I would have preferred, and it was a bit . . . stiff when I knew that it would all have to be given up; but that was nothing to . . . losing father. And besides, I think that I may get on in business and . . . help you, mother."

"Your father had set his heart on your being a doctor, and I don't know whether he ever spoke to you about it, but he hoped you might become a specialist—in surgery, I think; he said you had the hands at least for a good surgeon.

"It was his own heart's desire, you know, to be a surgeon, pure and simple, and Mr. Holman, the great consultant, considered him to be one of the best operators in the provinces, but he was obliged to be a general practitioner.

"Why? Oh, because he had no private means, and he had you and me to support, so he couldn't run any risks; he had to secure a regular income; and there is something I wish you to understand, in case you should ever think hardly of your father."

"Mother—as if I could! The very people in the street admired father; you know what they said in the *Morning Trumpet* about his self-sacrificing life, and his skill being at the disposal of the poorest, without money and without price."

"Yes, the papers were very kind, and his patients adored your father, but I am certain some of our neighbours criticised him because he did not make better provision for his wife and child. As if he had been extravagant or improvident, who never spent a farthing on himself, and was always planning for our welfare."

"You are just torturing yourself with delusions, I am sure, mater. Did any single person ever hint that father had not done . . . his duty by us? I can't believe it."

"One man did, at any rate, Jack, and that was our neighbour, Mr. Dodson."

"What did he say, the miserable old curmudgeon? Did he dare to bring a charge against father? I wish I had been with you."

"No, it was not that he said anything; it was

rather what he implied; he just questioned and questioned in an indirect fashion, all by way of interest in our affairs, but left the impression on my mind that he thought the doctor ought to have done better for his family."

"What business had Mr. Dodson to call at all and to ferret into our affairs, who was never before in our house? If we needed help—which we don't—he is the last man in this district to give it. Do you know he's the hardest, meanest creature in Liverpool? He'll leave a cab thirty yards from his house when he's coming from the station, to keep within the shilling limit, and he goes down in the penny 'bus with the workingwomen to save twopence."

"There is a certain young corn-broker," interpolated Mrs. Laycock, "who walks all the way to save even that penny, and I don't consider him mean."

"That is economy, and indicates the beginning of a fortune, which will be shared with a certain sarcastic mater. But Dodson is a millionaire, and has nobody depending on him but an old housekeeper. Certainly father was not economical by his standard."

"Your father was most careful and thrifty," said the widow eagerly, "and that is what I want to explain. He had to borrow money to educate himself, and that he paid back, every penny, with interest. Then, you know, a doctor cannot keep himself for the first few years of his practice—he only made £32 10s. 6d. the year he began—and when he reached £200 he did a . . . foolish thing."

"Let me guess, mater. Was it not marrying the dearest, sweetest, prettiest . . ."

"Hush, you stupid boy! And we had to keep up a certain appearance and pay a high rent, and we were very poor—poorer than the public ever knew.

"Of course, the doctor had a large practice before he died, and people used to think he made two and three thousand pounds a year; and Mrs. Tattler-Jones, who knows everything, said our income was £4,000.

"His last year, your father earned £1,800 and got in £1,200; the other £600 will never be paid; and yet he was so pleased because he had cleared off the last penny of his debt, and thought he would begin to lay something aside for your education."

"But why did he not get the other £600? Could the people not pay?"

"They could pay everybody else—wine merchants, jewellers, and car-owners—but their doctor's bill was left last, and often altogether, and your father would never prosecute."

. "And didn't father attend many people for nothing?"

"No one will ever know how many, for he did not even tell me; he used to say that if he didn't get often to church, he tried to do as people were told to do there; his commandment was the eleventh, 'Love one another.'"

"Did father believe the same as clergymen about things, mater?"

"No, not quite, and I suppose some people would call him a heretic; but you and I know, Jack, that if to do good and to be quite selfless, and to be high-minded, pure, and true, is to be like Christ, then the doctor was a Christian, the best I ever saw."

"Very likely he was the same sort of heretic as Christ Himself. I say, mater, there will be a good lot to speak up for father some day—widows and orphans and such like. I'm proud to be his son; it's a deal better to have such a father, of whom every person speaks well, than to come in for a pot of money. If old Dodson had a son, how ashamed he would be of his father."

"Money is not a bad thing, all the same, Jack," and Mrs. Laycock sighed. "If we had had a little more than the insurance policy, then we would not have had to come to this house, and you would not have been in an office."

"It's a jolly house, I think; and when the Christmas cards are stuck up the decorations will be complete. I wonder if the advance ones will come by this post? We'll see who remembers us."

"That's the bell; and see, six, seven, I declare, ten to begin with! Here's one in a rare old-fashioned hand. I'll take off the envelope and you will see the name. Why, it's a letter, and a long screed, and a . . . cheque!"

"Have some of those thieves paid their account? You are crying, mater. Is it about father? May I see the letter, or is it private?"

"No, it's about you, too, my son. I wish you would read it aloud; I'm not . . . quite able."

"LIVERPOOL, *December* 24, 189—.
"DEAR MADAM,—

"Along with many others in Liverpool, I experienced a feeling of keen regret that in the inscrutable actings of Providence your respected husband, Dr. Laycock, was, as it appears, prematurely removed from his work and family.

"It must be a sincere consolation for his widow to know that no man could have rendered more arduous and salutary service to his fellows, many of whom he relieved in pain, not a few of whom he was instrumental in restoring to their families from the portals of death. Without curiously inquiring into the affairs of private life, many persons were persuaded that Dr. Laycock was in the custom of attending persons of limited means as an act of charity, whereby he did much good, won much affection, and doubtless has laid up for himself great riches in the world to come, if we are to believe the good Book.

"I have not, however, sent you this letter merely to express my sympathy, shared with so many who have the privilege, denied to me, of your personal friendship, or to express the admiration felt by all for the eminent departed. My object is different, and must be its own excuse. Unless I have been incorrectly informed—and my authority seemed excellent—the noble life of Dr. Laycock hindered him from making that complete provision for his family which he would have desired, and which other men in less unselfish walks of life could have accomplished. This disability, I am given to understand, has seriously affected the career of your son, whom every one describes as a promising lad, so that he has been removed from a public school, and has been obliged to abandon the hope of entering on the study of medicine.

" If my information be correct, it was his father's wish that your son should follow in his steps, and it is incumbent on those who honoured Dr. Laycock for his example of humanity, to see that his cherished wish be fulfilled. Will you, therefore, in the light of the explanation I have made at some length, accept the draft I have the honour to send—value £1,000—and use the proceeds in affording to your son a complete medical education at home and abroad? The thought that the just desire of a good man has not fallen to the ground, and that a certain burden will be lifted from his widow's life, will be more than sufficient recompense to one whom you will never know, but who will, so long as he may be spared, follow your son's career with sincere interest.—Believe me, my dear madam, your obliged and grateful servant,

"ZACCHEUS."

"Hold it up against the light, mater; it's the prettiest Christmas card we'll ever see. . . . You ought to be laughing, and not crying. . . . But I feel a little—just a tiny wee bit watery myself.

"He might as well have told us his name; but I suppose he was afraid of a row. Zaccheus? Why, that's the man who gave the playgrounds. He must have a pile, and he knows how to use it; he's no Dodson, you bet. At any rate, though we don't know him, we can say, 'God bless him,' mater."

"Amen," said Mrs. Laycock. "I hope the father knows."

IV

"How do I know that there is something wrong, Bert? Because we've been married five years last month, and I can read your face like a book, or rather a great deal better than most books, for I'm not clever in following deep books, but I'm quite sure about your face.

"No, I don't imagine, for you may be able to hide what you feel on the 'Flags,' but you let out the secret at home; and that is one reason why I love you—because you are not cunning and secretive. Now tell me, is cotton down, and have you lost?

"Oh, yes, Bert, I know your principle, that a man ought to bear the burden outside, and the woman inside the home; but there are exceptions. You have acted up to your principle splendidly. You have never said a word all these years, although I know you've had anxious times, and you've helped me many a time with my little troubles. Let me help you in yours now."

"Queenie, if you want to put me to utter shame, you have taken the right way, for it's your thrift and good management which has given us our happy home, and I . . ."

"Yes, you, Bert, you have idled your time, I

suppose, and spent your money on dress, and generally neglected your family. For shame, sir, when you have done so well, and every one says that nobody is so much respected. Don't look like that if you love me. What is it?"

"It is necessary that you be told, and I was going to speak this evening, but it is very hard. Queenie, when I kissed the children and looked at you all so happy, I felt like a . . . murderer."

"Have you . . ."

"No, on my word of honour, I have done nothing wrong, *that* I can say; neither you nor the little ones have any cause to be ashamed of me."

"If you had, I would have stood by your side, Herbert, but I knew disgrace would never come by you; then what is it? If it's only the loss of some money, why, I know half a dozen economies."

"It's far worse than that, wife, I fear. This will be our last Christmas in our dear little home, and it's all my blame, and I feel . . . the basest of men. As if you had trusted me when I had deceived you all.

"You are the best wife ever man had. . . . I feel better, and I'll explain it all to you. It is not very difficult; it is so easy to be ruined.

"You know we are brokers, and our business is to buy or sell cotton for other people, and we are responsible for them, so that if they cannot pay the losses, we have to find the money.

"Two of our firms, which have been very kind

to us, were sure cotton would go up—and so it ought to have done, and will in the end—and they bought so many bales through us.

"Well, a big house, which can do pretty much as it likes, seized the opportunity of a fraud to rush in and upset the market, so our friends and many others have to face declines they cannot meet. So unless our poor little firm can pay £10,000 at least on Monday, we must stop, and . . . all our hard work to build up an honourable name is lost.

"We can scrape £4,000, and my partner and I have £1,000 private means to put in, and . . . that's all. £5,000 short.

"Yes, we have tried the Bank, but they can't do anything there. Goldsworthy, the manager, is the nicest fellow living, and his 'No' is almost as good as another's 'Yes'; but of course it was 'No'; we had no security; the cotton may go lower before it turns, and he has told us we must pay."

"But surely, Herbert, if the big firms knew how you were situated, they would help you, because things would come right in a few weeks, you say."

"Every man has to look after himself in the market. But I did go to Huddleston, because he has given me so much advice, and wanted me to take an interest in the Church. . . . I wish my tongue had been burned before I crossed his room.

"No, he wasn't rude—that's not his sin; he might be better if he were straighter. He hoped that I was prospering in business, and reminded me that I must not allow the world to get too much hold, and became eloquent on money being only a stewardship. But when I opened up my errand, he explained that he made it a principle never to lend money, and suggested that this was a chastening because we had hasted to be rich. He hoped that the issue would be sanctified, and . . . but I rose and left, quite sick."

"What a canting old wretch!" Mrs. Ransome was very angry. "I always hated that man's soft sawder; he's much too pussy to be true."

"He was not bound to help me unless he pleased. But what riled me was his religious talk; he might have spared me that at least. And if those operators who have knocked the market to pieces haul in £30,000, they will likely give £1,000 to missions.

"When a man has done his level best, and been fairly prudent, and has worked hard, and is getting a fair connection, and everything is taken away by a big, unscrupulous, speculative firm, which sees a chance of making a pile at the ruin of half a dozen struggling firms, it's a little hard."

"They ought to be put in jail; but they'll catch it some day;" and it was evident Mrs. Ransome, like many other people in her circumstances, found much satisfaction from the belief in future punishment.

"It's apt to make one bitter, too," Ransome went

on. "When I sat opposite old Dodson in the 'bus this afternoon—come to the penny 'bus now, you see, Queenie—looking out from below his shaggy eyebrows like a Scotch terrier, with meanness written over his shabby clothes, and almost heard the gold chinking in his pockets, and thought that he could save our home and secure my future by a cheque, and never miss the money—suppose he lost it, which he wouldn't if I lived—I declare, I could have . . . well, I did not feel as Christian as Huddleston would desire."

"Bert, have you ever thought what we would do if we became rich—how we would send flowers to people who were not well off, and let them use our carriage, and send overworked teachers and clerks for holidays, and . . ."

"Help lame dogs in cotton over stiles, eh, wifie? Yes, I've had my dreams too. I'd go in for the poor children's holiday fund, that would be my extravagance. But we are no better than other people. And were you never afraid that we would grow selfish and pompous, and mean and pharisaical, like Huddleston, and maybe end in being Dodsons?"

"No, no, that is impossible!" cried his wife, "because, for one thing, we have loved, and, perhaps, Mr. Dodson never was loved, poor soul; and if things come to the worst, remember there is a good deal left."

"There is something in that, Queenie; run over the inventory, and I'll check you."

"First of all there is you, the truest, kindest, bravest husband in Liverpool. . . ."

"Stop; that is your own private property, and we were to go over our common means; besides, the valuation is ninety per cent. too high."

"You be quiet. And there are two children, whom every one looks at in the street, and who are the sweetest . . . Nobody hears us, so it doesn't matter, and you know they are. Wouldn't it have been far worse if we had lost Reggie when he had diphtheria? Well, we have him and Maud, and they never looked better."

"That's true, wifie; go on; capital is mounting up."

"Then there's your good name, which has never been stained. Nobody says you are mean, or hypocritical, or unmanly, or . . . anything bad; and if . . . you can't pay that money on Monday, every person will know that it was not your fault, and that you will repay all you owe some day, if you can."

"Yes, please God, wife, we will. . . . You think too much of me, but go on."

"We have half a dozen friends, and, although they're not rich, they're true; and if we have to go into a smaller house and live very quietly, they won't mind; they'll just come closer, won't they?"

"Right again; you are getting on. We've somewhere about £50,000 working capital now."

"We have our books and our music, and . . .

five years of love and . . . spiritual blessings one doesn't talk about. . . ."

"One piece of property wanting, which is best of all—yourself, Queenie, surely the cleverest, loyalest . . ."

"You are talking nonsense now, Bert; and are you aware that it is past eleven o'clock? I'll turn out the gas in the dining-room if you will see that the door is fastened."

"Here is a letter which must have come by the last post and been forgotten; perhaps it's a Christmas card in advance. Let's see. Oh, I say, you've left me in darkness."

"Come up to our room; we can open it there; very likely it's a bill. Well?"

"I say . . . Queenie . . . no, it can't be a hoax . . . nobody would be so cruel . . . and here's an enclosure . . . letter from London bankers confirming . . . sit down here beside me; we'll read it together . . . so, as near as you can, and your arm round my neck . . . just a second before we begin . . . my eyes are . . . all right now."

"LIVERPOOL, *December* 22, 189—.

"DEAR SIR,—It has been my practice, as a man engaged for many years in commercial pursuits, to keep a watchful, and, I hope, not unkindly eye upon young firms beginning their business career in Liverpool. For the last five years I have observed your progress with much interest, and you will pardon my presumption and take no offence, when I express my satisfaction, as an old merchant, with your diligence, caution, ability, and, most of all, integrity, to which all bear witness.

"I was therefore greatly grieved to learn that your firm may be hardly pressed next week, and may be in danger of stoppage—all the more because I find no charge of folly can be brought against you, but that you are the indirect victims of one firm's speculative operations. There is no one, I am also informed, from whom you can readily obtain the temporary assistance you require and are morally entitled to receive.

"The only satisfaction I have in life is using such means as Providence has been pleased to put into my hands for the succour of people who are in every way better than myself, but who are in some kind of straits. I have therefore directed my London bankers to open an account for you and to put £10,000 to your credit. Upon this account you will be pleased to draw such a sum as will tide you over the present crisis, and such other sums as will enable you to extend your business along the safe and honourable lines you have hitherto followed. I do not doubt that you will repay the said sum or sums to the same account as you may be able to —no interest will be accepted—and I only lay one other obligation on your honour, that you make no endeavour to discover my name.

"Be pleased to accept my best wishes of this season for your admirable wife, your two pleasing children, and my confident hope for your final and large success in business.—I remain, your faithful friend,
"ZACCHEUS."

"Let us go and kiss the children, hubbie, and then . . . we might say the Lord's Prayer together."

V

"A respectable, elderly woman, did you say, Marshall?" said Mr. Greatheart in his room at the office; "certainly, bring her in. Very likely a widow wishing to get her son admitted to the Bluecoat School, or some poor householder in trouble about her taxes." For to this man came all sorts and conditions of people in their distresses, and to each he gave patient audience and practical succour.

"You don't trouble me. If I can be of any use, nothing will please me better," he said, placing a chair and making a kindly fuss to cover his visitor's confusion. "Now sit down and tell me all about it." That was why the respectable poor loved him, from the Catholic Irish of Scotland Road to the Orangemen of Toxteth.

"Is it your husband or your son you are so anxious about?"—for she was much agitated. "I notice that a woman hardly ever comes about herself. It's we men who are selfish, not the women."

"No, it's neither, for I am an unmarried woman. It's about my master, whom I believe you know, sir, Mr. Dodson."

"Samuel Dodson, you mean; I should think so! Have known him for fifty years—since we served our time together in Palmer's shipping office. What, is he ill?"

"He's dead . . . this morning. You'll excuse me, I was his housekeeper for near thirty year, and . . . I'm a little upset."

"Good gracious! No wonder. Maria Wilkins, did you say? . . . You may well be upset. And thirty years with him! Tell me how this happened, for we've heard nothing in the city. He couldn't have been ill long."

"No, sir, he was never ill at all—not what you would say proper; but I've seen him failin' for some time—gettin' thin like and growin' down—and last night he was that white and shaky, that I wanted him to see a doctor. But no, he wouldn't. If it had been me or the girl, he would have had a doctor when there was nothing wrong with us, he was that concerned about other people; but for himself . . ."

Mr. Greatheart nodded—indicating that Mr. Dodson's unselfish character was well known to him.

"'No, no, Maria,' says he, 'a doctor can do no good to me. I'm a tough old fellow'—speaking that way to me, being long with him—' I'll be all right to-morrow.' But I made bold to put a glass of brandy in his room, and pleaded with him to ring the bell if he was unwell—he was not easily managed—and that was all I could do, sir."

Her hearer was of opinion that from what he knew of Mr. Dodson's native obstinacy, Maria Wilkins had done all in the power of mortal woman, and possibly, more, than could have been accomplished by any man.

"Twice during the night I rose and listened at his door—his face, when he said good-night, lyin' heavy on me, so to say—and I heard nothing; but when he didn't answer in the mornin' I took it on me to open the door. Mr. Dodson was a-sittin' up in his bed, and at the sight of his face I knew how it was, havin' seen death many times. My old master . . . was gone," and the housekeeper yielded to her feelings.

"Dear, dear! So Sam Dodson is gone; an able and successful merchant, one who always met his obligations, and whose word was as good as his bond; he had a warmer heart than any person knew. I've seen a look in his face at a time, and am sure that he did good in his own way."

"God bless you for that, sir! but it's what I could have looked for from you, if I may say it without offence. And you never spoke a truer word, and that I can testify as has lived with master for a lifetime, and could tell the difference between the outside and the inside."

"Ah, yes, you saw the real man, Maria, but he was sometimes . . . well, hidden from the public."

"He had his peculiarities, and 'oo hasn't I say? Now, my wages when I came to him was just fourteen pounds, and they're just fourteen yet; but every Christmas, for many a year, master slipped a ten-pound note into my hand. 'Put that into your bank, Maria,' he would say, 'and never tell anybody you've got it.'

"As for food, he was aggravatin', for he would have nothing as was not plain, and he would check the books to a ha'penny; but if you was ill, why, he would bring home grapes with his own hand. We dare not for our lives give a morsel to beggars at the door, but if he heard of a poor family, nothin' would serve him but he would go and find out all about them."

"That's my Dodson, just as I imagined him," cried Mr. Greatheart; "tell me more, Maria; it's excellent, every word."

"Do you think he would let any person know he was givin' help? Not he; and he was artful, was master. Why, I've known him send me with money to a clergyman, that he might give it, and his words were, 'No name, Maria, or we part; just a citizen of Liverpool.'"

"Dodson all over! shrewd and unassuming, and full of charity. Have you anything else to tell, Maria?"

"Well, sir, I do not know for certain, and it was not for me to spy on my master, but I'm much mistaken if many a one in the better class was not the better of Mr. Dodson in their troubles."

"How do you think that?" inquired Mr. Greatheart in huge delight.

"I've seen him read a letter maybe six times, and he would wipe his eyes through pleasure as I took it. You wouldn't believe, maybe, as master could be like that."

"I do, Maria. I declare it's what I expected. And what then?"

"He would walk up and down the room, and speak to himself, and read another bit, and rub his hands . . ."

"I wish I had been there, Maria."

"And he would carry a letter like that in his pocket for days, and then he would put it carefully in the fire; but I saw him take it out, half-burned, and read a corner again before he burned that letter."

"Maria, I cannot tell you how much obliged I am to you for coming to me, and giving me such a touching account of your dear master. Now, is there anything I can do for you in this loss?"

"Lord bless me, sir, that I should have been taking up your time like this, and you a magistrate, and never told you what brought me! It's more than a month past that master said to me, 'Maria, if anything happens to me go to Mr. Greatheart's office, and give him my keys, and ask him to open my desk. He is a good man, and he's sure to come.'"

"Did he say so? That was most generous of him, and I appreciate it highly. I will come instantly, and shall bring a lawyer with me, a kind-hearted and able man. Good-bye for the present, Maria; you have fulfilled your charge, as I believe you have all your duty, excellently . . . excellently."

"You see, Welsby," as they went up to the house, "Dodson had left his firm, and had few friends, perhaps none—a reserved man about himself, but a true man at the bottom."

"So you have always said, Mr. Greatheart. We'll know now; my experience as a lawyer proves that, as a rule, a man's papers reveal him, and there are some curious surprises."

"If you look through that safe, and note the contents, Welsby, I'll read this letter addressed to me. I gather that I must be executor, and there seems to be no lawyer; very like Dodson, very—do everything for himself."

"LIVERPOOL, *April* 15*th*, 188—.
"BARNABAS GREATHEART, ESQ.

"MY DEAR SIR,—You will peruse this letter after my death, and you will be pleased to consider it as intended for your eyes alone, since it is in the nature of a confession.

"My early career was a continuous struggle with narrow and arduous circumstances, and I suffered certain disappointments at the hands of friends which I considered undeserved. In consequence of these experiences I grew penurious, cynical, merciless, hopeless, and, let me say it plainly, a sour, hard man, hating my neighbours, and despised of them. May the Almighty forgive me!

"This year in which I write, a great change has come over me, and my heart has been softened and touched at last with human sympathy. The force which has affected me is not any book nor sermon, but your example of goodness and your charity towards all men. In spite of the general judgment on me, which has been fully merited, I have seen that you do not shun me, but rather have gone out of your way to countenance me, and I have heard that you speak kindly of me. It is not my nature to say much; it is not yours to receive praise; but I wish you to know you have made me a new man.

"It seemed to me, however, dangerous that I should begin to distribute my means openly among charities, as I was inclined to do, since I might pass from hardness to pride and be charged with ostentation, as I had been once with miserliness, with sad justice in both cases.

"So it came to me that, still retaining and maintaining my character for meanness—as a punishment for my past ill-doing, and a check on vanity—I would gradually use my capital in the private and anonymous aid of respectable people who are passing through material adversity, and the help of my native city, so that my left hand should not know what my right was doing. This plan I have now, at this date, pursued for six months, and hope to continue to my death, and I did not know so great joy could be tasted by any human being as God has given to me. And now, to all the goodness you have shown me, will you add one favour, to wind up my affairs as follows:—

" (1) Provide for my housekeeper generously.

" (2) Give a liberal donation to the other servant.

" (3) Bury me quietly, without intimation to any one.

" (4) Distribute all that remains, after paying every debt, as you please, in the help of widows, orphans, and young men.

" (5) Place a packet, marked 'gilt-edged securities,' in my coffin.

" And consider that, among all your good works, this will have a humble place, that you saved the soul of—Your grateful friend,

"SAMUEL DODSON."

"What Dodson has done with his money, Mr. Greatheart, I don't know; all the securities together don't amount to £5,000. He seems to have been living on an annuity."

"His wealth is here, Welsby, in this packet of cancelled cheques, two hundred and eighty-seven, which go with him to the other side; and I tell you, Welsby, I know no man who has invested his money so securely as Samuel Dodson. See, read that top check."

"To Goldbeater, London, £10,000. Why the

draft I got for playgrounds was on that bank, and the date corresponds. Curious."

"Eh? What? You don't mean to say that this man we slanged and . . . looked down on was . . ."

"Yes, Zaccheus was Sam Dodson."

"I'ven seen him read a letter maybe six times, a citizen of Liverpool,'"

SAVED BY FAITH

SAVED BY FAITH

I

"So you have agreed to accept seven-and-sixpence in the pound from Hatchard?" Oxley said in his slow, quiet manner, as he smoked with his two friends after luncheon at the Club. "I could not attend the meeting, but I hear that the affairs showed badly."

"Yes, we took the sum he offered, and of course it would have done no good to put him in the Bankruptcy Court, as far as the dividend is concerned: very likely we should only have netted half-a-crown; but I had a good mind to refuse a composition." And in his excitement Beazley established himself for oratorical purposes on the hearthrug,—he had recently taken to municipal politics.

"You mean that Hatchard has acted foolishly, and ought not to have got into such a hole. I suppose you are right: Tommy was always a sanguine chap."

"Sanguine has nothing to do with it, Oxley, and I fancy you know that there's more than want of judgment at Hatchard's door. Of course the longest-headed men in the corn trade may make a mistake and be caught by a falling market, but that is no reason why a fellow should take in every friend he could lay hands on. What do you say, Macfarlane?"

That most phlegmatic and silent of Scots never said anything unless speech was absolutely necessary; and as the proposition that a man ought not to cheat his friends was one no person could deny, Macfarlane gave no sign.

"I'm afraid that it is a rather bad case," Oxley admitted with reluctance, "but I'm sorry for Tommy: when a man's at his wit's end he's apt to . . . forget himself in fact, and do things he would be the first to condemn at other times. A man loses his moral presence of mind."

Macfarlane indicated, after consideration, his agreement.

"That sounds very fine, Oxley," burst in Beazley, "but it's very dangerous doctrine and would cover some curious transactions. Hatchard knew quite well that when he was hopelessly bankrupt he ought not to have borrowed a thousand from Macfarlane and you and five hundred from me: our business losses were enough."

"Had none," murmured Macfarlane to himself.

"I was so angry," continued Beazley, "that I got hold of him afterwards in Fenwick Street and gave him as sound a talking to as ever a man got

SAVED BY FAITH

in this city: he'll not forget it in a hurry. You see he is a friend, and that makes me sore."

"Can you give us an idea what you said?" inquired Oxley drily, while Macfarlane showed that he was listening.

"Well, I said various things; but the gist was that his friends were ashamed of him—not about the cash, you know, but about the conduct, and that he was little better than a swindler: yes, I did."

Macfarlane smoked furiously.

"No, Oxley, he made no reply. Not one word of defence: he simply turned round and walked away. I suppose you think that I ought not to have been so hard on him?"

"Well, no doubt you did what seemed right, and Hatchard has not been quite straight; but I now understand what I saw two hours ago, and what gave me a shock. You favoured him with your mind about eleven, I should guess? Yes: then at twelve he came out of a restaurant in Dale Street as if he had been drinking. That is the first time Hatchard ever did that kind of thing, I believe, but it will not be the last: his face was quite changed —half woe-begone and half desperate."

"If Thomas takes to tasting"—Macfarlane was much moved—"it's all over with him: he's such a soft-hearted chap."

"Nonsense, you're making too much of it; but I was a trifle sharp, perhaps; he's been very provoking, and any other man would have said the same except you two fellows, and the one of you is so charitable that he would find an excuse for a pickpocket, and the other is so cannie that he can't make up his mind to say anything."

After which there was a pause.

"Yes," began Oxley again, falling into ancient history, "he has gone off form a bit—the best may do so at a time—but Tommy wasn't half a bad fellow once: he got a study at Soundbergh before me, and he was very decent with it, letting me do 'prep.' in it before exams.; and I never counted him sidey, did you, B.?"

"I should think not; I'll say that for him at any rate, there wasn't one scrap of humbug in Tommy: why, he was a prefect when I was in the fourth, and he didn't mind although a chap 'ragged' and chaffed him; he was the jolliest 'pre.' in the whole school. It was perhaps rather hard lines to slang him to-day,—I half wish I hadn't."

"If Tommy got a grub-box from home every chap in Buttery's house knew,"—Oxley was bent on reminiscences,—" it was shared round in three days, and his raspberry jam was not to be despised. I hear him yet: 'All right, Ox., dig in, there's lots left.' Now there's Byles, who makes speeches about hospitals: he was mean if you please."

"Mean ain't the word for Byles," and in his enthusiasm Freddie Beazley dropped into school slang, which no public-schoolboy ever forgets, and which lasts from generation to generation, like the speech of the Gypsies: " Byles was a beastly gut, and a sneak too; why, for all his cheek now he isn't fit to black Tommy's shoes. Tommy wasn't what you would call ' pie,' but he was as straight as a die. I'd give ten pounds not to have called him that word to-day." Freddie was breaking down.

"Poor old Tommy!" went on Oxley: "one never expected him to come such a cropper; he was a good all-round man—cricket, football, sports, Tommy did well for his house; he was a double-colour man."

"Do ye mind the ten miles, lads?" and Macfarlane chuckled.

"Rather," and Freddie could not sit still: "he did it in one hour twelve minutes and was it fifteen seconds?"

"Thirteen and three-fifths seconds." Macfarlane spoke with decision.

"And he could have walked back to Buttery's, as if he had never run a yard; but didn't the fellows carry him?"

"I had a leg myself." Macfarlane was growing loquacious.

"Yes, and he didn't swagger or brag about it," —Oxley took up the running,—"not he, but was just as civil as if he had won some footling little race at the low-country schools, where they haven't a hill within twenty miles, instead of running round Baughfell in the Soundbergh ten-mile."

"What did old Tommy do it for?" and Freddie Beazley almost wept at the thought that the crack of Soundbergh had played foul: "it couldn't be money; he was never selfish—as open-handed a chap as ever I saw."

"Wife and kids," answered Macfarlane, smoking thoughtfully.

"The Scot has it," said Oxley. "Tommy doesn't care one straw for himself, but he wanted, I take it, to keep that dear little wife of his comfortable and get a good education for his boys, and so he got deeper and deeper, trying to retrieve himself for their sakes. Mind you, I don't defend him, but that was his excuse; and now Tommy has gone under."

"Not if I can help it, boys," and Beazley's face flushed. "And I say, here are three of us: why shouldn't we join and—and—tighten the rope and haul Tommy on his feet again?"

Macfarlane took the briar root out of his mouth and regarded Freddie with admiration.

"We were all in the same house, and Tommy likes us, and we could do . . . that sort of thing when he wouldn't take it from others; and I say, it would be a jolly decent thing to do."

"You're all right, Freddie,"—Oxley was evidently pleased—"and we're with you" ("shoulder to shoulder," said Macfarlane, lighting his pipe with ostentatious care). "Now the first step is to let Tommy know that we have not turned our backs on him: my idea is that if he knows we three are going to stand by him he'll not throw up the sponge."

"Look here," cried Beazley, "I'll go round this minute, and I'll beg his pardon for what I said, and I'll tell him that we haven't forgotten the old days among the hills, and that we know he's a white man, and . . . in fact he'll take the cup yet."

"That will help mightily; and now let us make up our plans," said Oxley.

And that was how three men joined in a conspiracy for the business and social and personal salvation of Thomas Hatchard.

II

"How late you are, Tom—eight o'clock—and how tired you look, poor fellow! I've been thinking about you all day. Was it very trying this morning, or were they nice? They ought to have been, for everybody must know that it wasn't your fault."

"No, I don't think everybody could know that, Amy dear, for I don't know it myself, and some men have good reason to know the opposite. Well, yes, I was . . . rather sick at the meeting, and worse afterwards."

"Did they dare to insult you, Tom? If they had had one spark of gentlemanly feeling they would have pitied you. Do you mean that they . . . said things? Tell me, for I want to share every sorrow with you, darling."

"One man was very hard on me, and I didn't expect it from him—no, I won't tell you his name, for he behaved very handsomely in the end. Perhaps I didn't deserve all the sharp words, but I am sure I haven't deserved any of the kind words that were said before the day was done. But never mind about me just now: tell me how you got on. Wasn't it your visiting day? did . . . any one call?"

"So you were thinking about me in all your troubles!"—his wife put her arm round Hatchard's neck—"and you were afraid I should be deserted because you were victimised by those speculators! Now confess."

"Well, you know, Amy, society is not very merciful, and I think women are the cruelest of all. What hits a man, if he is unfortunate, or . . . worse, is that his poor wife is made to suffer. If her husband has done . . . I mean has acted foolishly, well, say, has lost money, his wife is neglected and cut and made to feel miserable. It's a beastly shame, and I was afraid that——"

"I would be sitting all alone to-day, because we are poor. Do you know, Tom, I was just a tiny bit nervous too, although I would not have told you this morning for worlds. And now I have splendid news to give you: our friends are as true as steel. Now answer a question, Tom, to see whether you and I agree about the difference between acquaintances and friends. Mention the names of the three families you would expect to stand by us in our trial."

"The Oxleys, of course, wife, and . . . I would have said the Beazleys, and, let me see, yes, the Macfarlanes, although their manner doesn't allow them to show what they feel. Am I right?"

"To a man (and woman), they all called to-day—the women, I mean: I daresay the men called on you. And they all said the nicest things, and what is best they said the nicest things about you: yes, they did, and if you doubt my word we shall separate . . . do you really think I would chaff to-day?

"Sit there, just where I can lay my head on your shoulder, and I shall describe everything. It was half-past two when I began to watch the clock and wonder whether any one would come: have other people had the same feeling? About a quarter to three the bell rang, and my heart beat: who would it be? It was nothing—a tax paper; and I began to think what I would have done if the same thing had happened to one of our friends—how I would have simply rushed along and been in the house the first decent minute after lunch, and how I would——"

"I know you would, Pet, and that is why they did it to you. Well, drive on."

"Exactly at eight minutes to three—oh, I know the time to-day without mistake—the door opened, and in came Mrs. Macfarlane; and do you know what she did?"

"She didn't!" cried Hatchard—"not kissed you?"

"Yes, she did, and a real kiss; and she took me in her arms, and I saw tears in her eyes, and—and . . . I cried for a minute; I couldn't help it, and it was quite a comfort. She hadn't said a word all this time, and that was just right, wasn't it?"

"I'll never say a word against the Scots' manner again," said Tom huskily.

"But she spoke quite beautifully afterwards, and told me of some trials no one knows, which they had ten years ago, and how they had never loved one another so much before. When reticent people give you their confidence it touches your heart, and we used to think her voice harsh, and to laugh at her accent."

"God forgive me!" said Thomas: "I'm a fool."

"She said: 'You know how quiet Ronald is, and how he hardly ever gets enthusiastic. Well, it would have done you good to have heard him speak about Mr. Hatchard this morning. He said——'"

"Don't tell me, Amy—it . . . hurts; but I'm grateful all the same, and will never forget it. And who came next?"

"Mrs. Oxley; and what do you think? We are to have their house at Hoylake for August, so the chicks will have their holiday. Mr. Oxley has been quite cast down, she says, about you, for he has such a respect——"

"It's good of them to think about the children, but never mind about me."

"You are very unfeeling, Tom, to stop me at the best bits, when I had saved them up and committed them to memory: perhaps you would get vain, however, and become quite superior. What do you think of your ' kindness,' and your ' generosity,' and your ' popularity,' and your ' straightness ' ? You are shivering: are you cold?"

"No, no; but you haven't told me if Mrs. Beazley was kind to you: did she call between four and five?"

"Yes: how did you know the hour?"

"Oh, I . . . guessed, because she . . . was last, wasn't she?"

"She apologised for being so late; indeed, she was afraid that she might not get round at all, but I'm so glad she came, for no one was more glowing about you: I saw, of course, that she was just repeating Mr. Beazley's opinion, for every one can see how he admires . . .

"Tom, you are very ungrateful, and for a punishment I'll not tell you another word. What is wrong? has any one injured you? Was it Mr. Beazley?"

"Beazley said kinder things in my office to me, in difficult circumstances too, than I ever got from any man: some day, Amy, I'll tell you what he said, but not now—I cannot—and he spent two hours canvassing for business to start me as a corn broker, and he . . . got it."

"It could not be Mr. Oxley."

"Oxley has given me a cargo to dispose of, and I never had any of his broking before; and he told me that some of my old friends were going to . . . to . . . in fact, see me through this strait, speaking a good word for me and putting things in my way.

"Yes, of course Macfarlane came to the office, and said nothing for fifteen minutes: just gripped my hand and smoked, and then he rose, and as he was leaving, he merely mentioned that Beazley and Oxley had become securities for £5,000 at the bank; he is in it, too, you may be sure."

"How grateful we ought to be, Tom dear; and how proud I am of you!—for it's your character has affected every person, because you are so honourable and high-minded. Tom, something *is* wrong; oh, I can't bear it: don't cry . . . you are overstrung . . . lie down on the couch, and I'll bathe your forehead with eau de Cologne."

"No, I am not ill, and I don't deserve any petting; if you knew how mean I have been you would never speak to me again. If they had scolded me I would not have cared; but I can't bear their kindness.

"Amy, you must not send for the doctor, else you will put me to shame; my mind is quite right, and it isn't overwork: it's . . . conscience: I am not worthy to be your husband, or the friend of these men."

"You will break my heart if you talk in this way. You unworthy! when you are the kindest, truest, noblest man in all the world—don't say a word— and everybody thinks so, and you must let us judge.

Now rest here, and I'll get a nice little supper for you," and his wife kissed him again and again.

"It's no use trying to undeceive her," Hatchard said to himself when she was gone; "she believes in me, and those fellows believe in me—Freddie more than anybody, after all he said; and please God they will not be disappointed in the end."

III

"You've got here before me, Mac.," cried Freddie Beazley, bursting into Oxley's private room, "and I simply scooted round. Oh, I say, you've broken every bone in my hand, you great Scotch ruffian: take the ruler out of his fist, Ox., for heaven's sake, or else he'll brain us.

"Ox., you old scoundrel, read that letter aloud. Mac. wasn't a creditor—he wishes he was this day—and he doesn't know it verbatim, and I'm not sure about a word or two. Stand up, old man, and do the thing properly. There now, we're ready."

July 7, 1897.

"DEAR SIR,—

"It will be in your recollection that in July, 1887, I was obliged to make a composition with my creditors while trading as a corn merchant under the style of Thomas Hatchard & Co., and that they were good enough to accept the sum of seven shillings and sixpence in the pound.

"Immediately thereafter, as you may be aware, I began business as a corn broker, and owing to the kind assistance of certain of my creditors and other friends have had considerable success.

"Having made a careful examination of my affairs, I find that I can now afford to pay the balance of twelve shillings and sixpence which is morally due to my creditors of 1887, and it affords me much personal satisfaction to discharge this obligation.

"I therefore beg to enclose a cheque for the amount owing to you, with 5 per cent. compound interest, and with sincere gratitude for your consideration ten years ago.

"I have the honour to remain,
"Your obedient servant,
"THOMAS HATCHARD."

"Isn't that great, young gentlemen?" and Beazley took a turn round the room: "it's the finest thing done in Liverpool in our time. Tommy has come in again an easy first on the ten miles—just skipped round Baughfell: there's nothing like the old school for rearing hardy fellows with plenty of puff in them for a big hill."

"Thomas 'ill be a proud man the night," remarked Macfarlane, "and his wife will be lifted."

"What about the Hatchard securities and encouragement company? isn't it a booming concern, and aren't the three men lucky dogs who took founder's shares? Oxley, old chap," and Freddie grew serious, "it was you who put Tommy on his legs, and helped him on to this big thing."

"Nonsense! we all had a share in the idea; and now that I remember, it was you, Beazley, who sang his praises that day till Macfarlane allowed his pipe to go out, and I had to join the chorus. Isn't that so, Mac.?"

Macfarlane was understood to give judgment of strict impartiality—that the one was as bad as another, and that he had been a victim in their hands, but that the result had not been destructive of morality in Liverpool, nor absolutely ruinous to the character of Thomas Hatchard, beyond which nothing more could be said. He offered the opinion on his own account that the achievement of Thomas had been mighty.

"You can put your money on that, Mac.," and Beazley went off again: "to pay up the balance of that composition and every private loan with interest, compound too, is simply A1. T. H. has taken the cake. And didn't he train for it, poor chap!

"No man enjoyed a good cigar more than Tommy—could not take him in with bad tobacco. Well, I happen to know that he hasn't had one smoke since July 7th, '87. Of course he could have had as much 'baccy as he wanted; but no, it was a bit of the training—giving up every luxury, d'ye see?"

"I wish I was Thomas the night," remarked Macfarlane. "He 'ill have a worthwhile smoke."

"He rather liked a good lunch, and did justice to his grub, too," continued Beazley. "Well, for ten years he's taken his midday meal standing, on milk and bread—not half bad all the same—at the Milk-Pail in Fenwick Street, and he wouldn't allow himself a cup of tea. You saw how he lived at Heswall, Oxley?"

"Yes, he found out that he could get a little house, with a bit of garden, for forty pounds, taxes included, and so he settled there and cut the whole concern here. There was one sitting-room for the children and another for themselves, and the garden was the drawing-room; but I don't believe Hatchard was ever happier, and Mrs. Hatchard has turned out a heroine."

"Tommy played up well," broke in Beazley, "and he never missed a chance. There has not been any brokerage lying loose in the corn market these ten years, you bet; and what he got he did well. Do you hear that MacConnell of Chicago has given him his work to do? Tommy is steaming down the deep-water channel now, full speed. What's to be done? that's the question. We simply must celebrate."

"Well, replied Oxley, "I suppose the creditors will be giving him a dinner at the Adelphi and that sort of thing. But there's something Hatchard would like far better than fifty dinners. He has never entered the corn exchange since his failure, and I know he never would till he could look every man in the face. What do you say to ask Barnabas Greatheart to call at his office and take him?"

"Oxley, you are inspired, and ought to take to

politics: it's just the thing Greatheart would like to do, and it will please the men tremendously. I bet you a new hat there will be a cheer, and I see them shaking hands with Tommy: it will touch up two or three scallawags on the raw first-rate, too, who have made half a dozen compositions in their time. But what about ourselves, Ox.?"

"Aye," said Macfarlane; "we're not common shareholders in this concern: we're founders, that's what we are."

"I was thinking before you men came in that a nice piece of silver for their dinner-table—they will come up to town now—say a bowl with some little inscription on it. . . ."

"The very thing: we'll have it this afternoon; and, Ox., you draw up the screed, but for my sake, as well as Tommy's, put in something about honour, and, old fellow, let it be strong; it'll go down to his boys, and be worth a fortune to them, for it will remind them that their father was an honest man."

It is not needful to describe, because everybody in the Liverpool Corn Market knows, how Barnabas Greatheart came into the room arm in arm with Thomas Hatchard, and how every single man shook hands with Thomas because he had gone beyond the law and done a noble deed, and was a credit to the corn business; and how Tommy tried to return thanks for his health a week after at the Adelphi, and broke down utterly, but not before he had explained that he wasn't at all the good man they thought him, but that he happened to have had better friends than most men.

What is not known is that on the very evening of the great day a special messenger brought over to the cottage at Heswall a parcel, which, being opened, contained a massive silver bowl, with this inscription :—

TO
MRS. THOMAS HATCHARD,
FROM THREE FRIENDS,
IN ADMIRATION OF HER HUSBAND'S
BUSINESS INTEGRITY AND
STAINLESS HONOUR.
July 7, 1897.

and that on the first anniversary of the great day the Hatchards gave a dinner-party in their new house at Mossley Hill, where six guests were present, whose names can be easily supplied, and the bowl, filled with roses, stood in the centre of the table so that all could read the writing thereon; that without any direct allusion to the circumstances, or any violation of good taste, the bowl came into conversation eleven times: once in praise of the roses; once in discussion of the pattern (Queen Anne); once with reference to the pedestal of Irish bog-oak; once in verification of the fact that " honour " was spelt with a " u " (it was Freddie who, with much ingenuity, turned the search-

SAVED BY FAITH

light on honour); and seven times in ways too subtle and fleeting for detection. When the ladies left the room there was a look between the host and his wife as he held the door; and when the other men's cigars were fully lit, Tommy made and finished, with some pauses, a speech which may not sound very eloquent on paper, but which the audience will never forget. "There's a text somewhere in the Bible," he said, pretending that his cigar was not drawing—"which runs something like this, 'saved by faith,' and when I look at that bowl I remember that I . . . was saved that way; but it wasn't . . . my faith: it was the faith . . . of you three men."

THE LAST SACRIFICE

THE LAST SACRIFICE

I

Firelight casts a weird enchantment over an old-fashioned room in the gloaming, and cleanses it from the commonplace. Distant corners are veiled in a shadow full of mystery; heavy curtains conceal unknown persons in their folds; a massive cabinet, full of Eastern curios, is flung into relief, so that one can identify an Indian god, who distinctly grins and mocks with sardonic humour, although in daylight he be a personage of awful solemnity; a large arm-chair, curiously embroidered, grows into the likeness of a stout elderly gentleman of benevolent heart but fierce political prejudices; the flickering flames sketch on the ceiling scenes of past days which can never return; and on a huge mirror the whole interior is reflected as in a phantasmagoria.

"It is, I do honestly believe, the dreariest room in Bloomsbury, and one can hardly go farther," said a young woman, lying at her ease on the white bearskin before the fire; "and yet it has a beauty of its own—sober, of course, but kindly; yes, that is the word, and true. My room at Kensington, that Reggie and his artist friends have been doing up in their best style, as Maples say, does not look prettier to-night nor your lovely black oak at the Rectory."

"If you had got your will, Frances," answered a sister some six years older from the couch, "every stick of this furniture would have been sold long ago, and the walls draped in pale green. You are full of sentiment to-night."

"It's the double wedding and the departure from the ancestral mansion which is casting shadows over my too susceptible heart and a glamour over this prosaic old room with its solid Philistine furniture," and Frances pretended to conceal her rising emotion behind a fan. "Your already matronly staidness, Gerty, is incapable of entering into such moods. It is a mercy one daughter, at least,—I think there are two—reproduces mother, and can never be accused of sentiment—and such a blessing for the Rector! It is a rule, one would say from observation, that clergymen choose matter-of-fact and managing wives, as a check, I suppose, on their own unworldliness and enthusiasm. As for me, so frivolous and . . . affectionate, poor papa must have the entire responsibility," and Frances sighed audibly.

"Are you really deceived by mother's composure and reserve?" Gertrude's quiet tone emphasized the contrast between her refined face and Frances'

Spanish beauty. "Strangers count her cold as marble, and I can excuse them, for they judge her in society. We ought to know better, and she has always seemed to me the very type of loyalty and faithfulness."

"Of course she is the dearest mater ever was, and far too unselfish, and she has been most patient with her wayward youngest daughter; but she is —well, I could not say that she is a creature of emotion."

"You believe, I suppose,"—Gertrude was slightly nettled—" in women who kiss frantically on meeting, first one cheek and then the other, and sign themselves 'with a thousand remembrances and much love, yours most affectionately,' who adopt a new friend every month, and marry three times for companionship."

"Gertrude, I am ashamed of you; you are most provoking and unjust; my particular detestations, as you know very well, are a couple of girls' arms round each other's waists—studying one another's dresses all the time—and a widow who marries again for protection,—it's a widower who says companionship,—but I enjoy your eloquence; it will be a help to Fred when he is sermon-making. You will collaborate—that is the correct word, isn't it?"

"None of us will ever know how deep and strong is the mater's love," continued Gertrude, giving no heed to her sister's badinage; "she cannot speak, and so she will always be misunderstood, as quiet people are. Did you ever notice that she writes her letters on that old desk, instead of using the escritoire? that is because it was father's; and although she never mentions his name, I believe mother would rather starve than leave this house or part with a chair that was in it when he was living.

"Frances, I'll tell you something I once saw and can never forget. When I slept in mother's room, I woke one night, and found she had risen. She opened a drawer that was always kept locked, and took out a likeness of father. After looking at it again and again—can you believe that?—she laid it on a chair, and, kneeling down, prayed to God for us all, and that they might meet again; and then she looked at him once more, and put the picture in its place.

"Pray God, Frances, that you and I, who are to be married on Tuesday, may love as she has done, once for ever; do you know I've often thought that Grace is the only one of us that has mother's power of affection, and yet we are to be married and she is to be left."

"Yes, Grace is like mother, and yet I don't think mother understands her one bit. What a wife she would make to some man, Gertie; only it would be bad for him. She would serve him like a slave, and he would be insufferable.

"But there is no fear of that calamity," Frances went on, "for Grace will never marry. She is beginning to have the airs of an old maid already, a way of dressing and a certain primness which is alarming."

"It passes me," said Gertrude, "how no man has seen her excellence and tried to win her; do you know I've sometimes thought that Mr. Lennox admired her; they would certainly make a perfect pair."

"You are the dearest old stupid, Gertrude. Of course George Lennox adores Grace, as he would do a saint in a painted window; and Grace appreciates him because he teaches astronomy or conchology or something to working men in the East End. Neither of them knows how to make love; their conversation is a sort of religious exercise," and Frances' eyes danced with the delight of a mistress in her art. "Why, I once did my best with him just to keep my hand in, and, Gertrude, you might as well have flirted with that wretched god. I would rather have the god, for he winked to me just now quite distinctly, the reprobate old scoundrel."

"Perhaps you're right, and Grace does not wish to marry. But it will be lonely in this big empty house for mother and her when we are gone."

"Dull! Gertie, you do not understand the situation. It will be a relief for the two of them to have this love traffic over, and no more men about the house. Grace simply endures it, as a nun might, and the mater resents any of her daughters being married. They have their programme fixed. Grace will visit her sick people in the forenoon, and the mater will do her tradesmen; in the afternoon the two will attend the Committee for the Relief of Decayed Washerwomen, and after dinner Gracie will read to mother out of Hallam's *Middle Ages*.

"I'll box that creature's ears," and Frances jumped to her feet, a very winsome young woman indeed; "he's grinning from ear to ear on his pedestal at some wicked joke, or as if he knew a family secret. He's an old cynic, and regards us as a pair of children prattling about life."

II

"My work at Court was finished a little earlier to-day, and I have done myself the pleasure of calling to inquire for Mrs. Leconte and you after the marriage. Will you accept a few roses?" The manner was grave and a trifle formal, but George Lennox was one in whom any woman might safely put her trust—tall and well built, with a strong face and kindly eyes—a modest and courteous gentleman.

"It is good of you to remember us, but, indeed, you have always been most kind," said Miss Leconte, with the faintest flush on her cheek. "Mother is out, and will be sorry to have missed you. Will you not sit down, and I'll order tea."

The London sun, which labours hard, with many ingenuities, to do his part by every home and give to each its morsel of brightness, found the right angle at that moment, and played round Grace's face with soft afternoon light.

She was not beautiful like her sisters, but one man out of a thousand would learn to love her for the loyalty that could be read in the grey eyes, and the smile, a very revelation of tenderness, as if her soul had looked at you.

"Yes, mother and I have settled down to our quiet round after the festivities; mother needs a rest, for you know how little she thinks of herself; her unselfishness puts one to shame every day."

Mr. Lennox looked as if he knew another unselfish person, and Grace continued hurriedly:

"Every one thought the marriage went off so well, and the day was certainly perfect. Didn't Gertrude and Frances make lovely brides, each in her own way?"

"So the people said, and I know how they would look, but it happened that I stood where I could only see the bridesmaids."

"Will you excuse me putting the roses in water? they are the finest I've seen this summer, and I want to keep them fresh," and she escaped for the moment.

He watched her place one dish on the end of the grand piano and another on a table near her mother's chair, and a yearning look came over his face.

They talked of many things, but both were thinking of one only, and then it was she, in her kindness, that provoked the catastrophe.

"You will come again and see mother; she misses Gerty and Frances, and it is very pleasant to have a talk with old friends."

"And you, Grace—Miss Leconte, I mean—may I not come to visit you?"

"You know that I am glad when you come, and

always will be; you are my friend also," and she looked at him with frank, kind eyes.

"Nothing more than friend after all these years—seven now since first we met. Do you not guess what I was thinking as your sisters stood beside their bridegrooms in church?" But she did not answer.

"Can you give me no hope, Grace? If you told me to come back in five years, I would count them days for the joy of hearing you call me by my name at the end, as a woman speaks to the man she loves."

"You ought not to open this matter again," but she was not angry, "for my mind is made up, and cannot be changed. There is no man living whom I respect more; none to whom I would rather go in time of trouble; there is nothing I would not do for you, Mr. Lennox, except one——"

"But it is the one thing I desire"; and then Lennox began to plead. "No man is worthy of you, Grace, and I least of all. The world counts me proud and cold, and I regret my manner every day, but I can love, and I love you with all my heart. You know I can give you a house and every comfort of life—perhaps I may be able to bring you honour and rank some day; but these are not the arguments I would urge or you would care to hear. Love is my plea—that I never loved before I saw you, and if you refuse me, that I will not love any other.

"Do not speak yet." His face was white, and he stretched out his hands in appeal. "Have we not the same . . . faith and the same ideals? Could not we work together for a lifetime, and serve the world with our love? Perhaps I ought to have spoken years ago, but the Bar is an uncertain profession, and my position was not made. It seemed to me cowardly to ask a woman's love before one could offer her marriage, so I kept silent till last spring, when I saw your sisters' lovers and their happiness—and then I could not help telling you that one man hoped to win your heart. Now I ask for your answer.

"If you love another man," he went on, "or feel that you can never love me, tell me at once, Grace, for this were better for us both. I would never cease to love you, for we slow, cold men do not change, and if you had need I would serve you, but never again would I . . . trouble you," and the ablest of the junior counsel at the Chancery Bar broke down before a girl that had no other attraction than the goodness of her soul.

Grace Leconte was the calmest of the two when she spoke, but her face was set like a martyr's in his agony.

"I had hoped, Mr. Lennox, that you would not have followed up what you said in March, but yet so selfish is a woman, I am not sorry to be told that I . . . am loved by such a man.

"Believe me, it is I that am unworthy. You

have made too much of a very ordinary woman. But I am proud of . . . your love, and in after years, when I find the strain too heavy, will often say, 'God has been good to me. George Lennox loved me.'"

He was waiting anxiously, not knowing how this would end.

"You have spoken frankly to me, and have laid bare your heart," she went on. "I do not see why I should be hindered by custom from telling you the truth also," and then she hesitated, but only for a little. "For years—I do not know how long—I have . . . loved you, and have followed your career as only a woman who loves could—gathering every story of your success, and rejoicing in it all as if you had been mine. Wait, for I have not yet done.

"If I could say 'Yes,' I would, George—may I call you this, only to-day?—without any delay, but I must say 'No' instead, although it may break my heart. I can never be your wife."

"What do you mean . . . ?"

"Bear with me, and I will tell you all. You know now it is not because I do not want to marry you—I do; I also can love, and I do not wish to be an old maid—no woman does. I will not pretend indifference, but it is not possible for me to leave my mother."

"Is that all?" cried Lennox, as one who has cast off a great dread. "I would never ask Mrs.

Leconte to part from the last of her daughters. She will come with you, and we shall strive to make her life peaceful and glad. . . ."

"Please do not go on, for this can never be. No power could induce mother to change her way or live with us. She will live and die alone, or I must stay with her. My duty is clear, and, George, you must . . . accept this decision as final."

"You will let me speak to her and put our case . . .?"

"No, a thousand times, no. She must never know our secret. It would still be the same between you and me, but mother would fret every year because I had made this sacrifice. As it is she knows nothing, and will never guess the truth. Promise me you will say nothing; that is one favour I have to ask, and there is another, that . . . you do not call again, for I could not bear to see you for a little . . . for some years. You will do so much for me, will you not?"

He had sat down, his head on his breast, a figure of utter dejection, when she laid her hand on his arm.

"Things cannot end after this fashion," and Lennox sprang to his feet; "does not the Book say that a man will forsake father and mother for love's sake, and should it not be so with a woman also? What right have you to deny your love and blight two lives?"

"Many would say that I am wrong, but my mind

is made up. Do not try me farther, George; God knows how hard it is to obey my conscience. My duty, as I see it, and that is all one can go by, is to mother, and if I made it second even to love, I should be inwardly ashamed, and you . . . you could not respect me.

"Say you understand," and her lips trembled; "say that you forgive me for the sorrow I have brought upon you, and let us say farewell."

He made as though he would have clasped her in his arms and compelled her to surrender, and then he also conquered.

"God keep and bless you, Grace; if I cannot have you in my home, none can keep me from carrying you in my heart," and he was gone.

She watched him till he disappeared round the corner of the square, and noticed that he walked as one stricken with age. One of their windows commanded a corner of the square garden, where the trees were in their first summer greenery, and she could hear the birds singing. As she turned away, the sunlight lingered on the white roses which George Lennox had brought as the token of his love, and then departed, leaving the faded room in the shadow.

III

"This frame seems to have been made for our purpose, Grace," and Mrs. Leconte arranged in order Gertrude with her two girls and Frances with her two boys. "It seems only a few months, instead of four years, since the wedding day.

"They have good husbands and happy homes. I only wish their father . . ." This was so unusual that Grace looked at her mother, and Mrs. Leconte checked herself. "You are going down to the Rectory, I hope, next week; Gertrude is always anxious to have you, and August in London is very trying."

"Certainly; but on one condition, mother, that you go too; it would be such a joy to Gerty, and you must have some change."

"Perhaps I will, a little later, but I never leave London in August. I have always been very strong, and I like a . . . quiet time then."

"Mother," and Mrs. Leconte turned at the passion in her daughter's voice, "why will you not allow any of us to share your remembrance and your grief? We know why you shut yourself up alone in August, and now, when there are just you and I, it hurts me that I may not be with you, if it were only to pray . . . or weep. Would it not be some help?" and Grace took her mother's hand, a very rare caress.

"You are a good daughter, Grace," she spoke with much difficulty, "but . . . God made me to be alone, and silent. I was not able to tell either joy or sorrow even to your father. You spoke of weeping; do you know I've never shed a tear since I was a child—not often then.

"When he died, my eyes were dry. . . . Oh, Grace, you are most like me: may God deliver you from a tearless grief; but it must be so with me to the end."

"Dearest mother," said Grace, but she did not kiss her.

"You are often in my thoughts, Grace," after a long silence, "and I am concerned about you, for you have aged beyond your years. Are you . . . well?"

"What a question, mater; you know that I have the health of a donkey—save a headache now and then that gives me an interesting pallor. You forget that I am getting to be an old maid, nearly thirty."

"Is it really that . . . I mean do you not feel lonely—it is a contrast, your sisters' lot and yours, and a woman's heart was made for love, but if it be so do not sorrow over much . . . I can't explain myself—there are many in this world to love, and, at any rate . . . you will never know the sense of loss."

"That is the postman's ring," and Grace made an errand to obtain the letters, and lingered a minute on the way.

"Only one letter, and it's for you, mother. I think I know the handwriting."

"Of course you do; it's from Mrs. Archer, George Lennox's aunt. She is a capital correspondent, and always sends lots of news. Let me see. Oh, they've had Gertrude and her husband staying a night with them for a dinner.

"'Everything went off well' . . . 'Gerty looked very distinguished, and has just the air of a clergyman's wife.' Gerty was always suited for that part, just as Frances does better among the painters. . . . I wish all the same they were both here, Grace, but I suppose that's a wrong feeling, for marriage is a woman's natural lot . . . that is in most cases, some have another calling.

"Do you know who has been staying with the Archers? Why, you might guess that—George Lennox; he's Jane Archer's favourite nephew, and I don't wonder; no woman, I mean sensible woman, could help liking him; he's so reliable and high-toned, as well as able, and do you know, I always thought Mr. Lennox good-looking.

"What's this? 'You will be sorry to hear that

George is looking very ill indeed, and just like an old man, and he's not forty yet.' Are you there, Grace? Oh, I thought perhaps you had left the room. Isn't that sad about Mr. Lennox?

"Mrs. Archer goes on to say that he overworks shockingly, and that he is bound to break down soon; he will take no advice, and allows himself no pleasure. What a pity to see a man throwing away his life, isn't it?"

"Perhaps he finds his . . . satisfaction in work, mother."

"Nonsense; no man ought to kill himself. Mr. Lennox ought to have married years ago, and then he would not have been making a wreck of himself; I don't know any man who would have made a better husband, or of whom a woman would have been prouder." And Mrs. Leconte compelled a reply.

"He is a good man, and I think you are right, mother." Something in her tone struck Mrs. Leconte's ear.

"Grace, Mr. Lennox used to come frequently to this house, and now I have noticed he never calls."

Her daughter said nothing.

"It was after your sisters' wedding that he ceased to call. Do you think . . . I mean, was he in love with Gerty? Frances it couldn't be. I never thought of that before, for I am not very observant. Nothing would have given me more pleasure, if my daughters were to be married, than to have George Lennox for a son-in-law. Can it be, Grace, that Gerty refused him, and we have never known?"

"I am sure she did not, mother"; and again Mrs. Leconte caught a strange note in her daughter's voice.

"Do you know, I suspect that if you had given him any encouragement, George Lennox would have been a happy man to-day. Is that so, Grace?

"Pardon me, Grace, perhaps I ought not to ask such a question; it came suddenly into my mind. Whatever you did was no doubt right; a woman cannot give her hand without her heart even to the best of men. If it be as I imagine, I do not blame you, Grace, but . . . I am sorry for George Lennox."

Grace wept that night over the saddest of all the ironies of life—a sacrifice which was a mistake and which had no reward.

AN EVANGELIST

AN EVANGELIST

His private business was lard, which he bought for the rise and sold for the fall—being a bull or a bear without prejudice—and with a success so distinguished that his name was mentioned in highly complimentary terms on the American market. When the famous lard corner of 1887 had been wound up, and every man had counted his gains (or losses), old man Perkins, of Chicago, did justice to his chief opponent, like the operator of honour that he was.

"No, sir, I ain't a slouch, and the man who says that I don't know lard is a mining expert; but Elijah Higginbotham, of Victoria Street, Liverpool, Great Britain, has come out on top: he's a hustler from way back, is Elijah."

Mr. Perkins' opinion, which was a deduction based on the results of at least six first-class encounters, was generally accepted on both sides of the Atlantic, and it was conceded that what Mr. Elijah Higginbotham did not know about that capricious and volatile instrument of speculation was not knowledge. As a matter of principle he was opposed to gambling, and denounced it with much eloquence and perfect sincerity at conferences of a religious character,—warning his audience, composed mainly of old ladies, against the Derby—but if this evil and ruinous spirit should happen to enter his market, where it seemed quite at home, Elijah was prepared to overthrow gambling with its own weapons, and on such occasions it was worldly wisdom to bet on Elijah's side. His ideas regarding the date of unfulfilled prophecy might be crude, but his foresight regarding the future of lard was an instinct.

His public business was religion, and especially the work of an evangelist, and to this Elijah gave himself with incredible courage and diligence. When he was not manipulating lard or asleep, he was inquiring into the condition of his neighbour's soul, and none could escape him. It was freely told on 'Change how he had fallen on an alderman, who had responded too generously to the loyal toasts at a municipal banquet, and so impressed him with the shortness of life and the awfulness of the future, that the worthy man was bathed in tears, and promised if spared to join the Plymouth Brethren next day. Bishops of the Church, who are awful beings to ordinary people, and with whom some of us hardly dare to speak about the weather, were to Elijah a chosen prey in railway carriages, so that he would hunt a train to travel with one for a long journey, and he has been known to reduce one pompous prelate to the verge of apoplexy by showing before a (secretly) delighted company of "firsts" that this successor to the Apostles did not really know wherein conversion consisted, and, by not very indirect inference, that the Bishop was himself still unconverted. Unto Elijah belongeth also the doubtful and perilous distinction of having been the unwilling and (as he would himself say) unworthy means of stopping a London express when going at full speed. It was, of course, an old and perhaps over-nervous gentleman who actually pulled the cord and waved to the guard, and it was Elijah who offered immediate and elaborate explanations; but Elijah's fellow-passenger held a strong position when he laid the blame on Elijah.

"It's well enough for him to say that he was speaking spiritually, but he told me plainly that I was going to Hell, and not to London, and I put it to you, guard,"—by this time there was a large jury of interested passengers,—"when the only other man in the compartment uses language of that kind, and he much younger and stronger, whether I wasn't justified in calling for assistance."

Quiet men, not prone to panics, just breaking upon their luncheon at the Club, rose and fled when Elijah sat down at the same table, knowing well that not only would a forbidding silence be no protection, but that even ingenious and ensnaring allusions to the critical condition of the lard market would be no protection against personal inquiries of the most searching character. He was always provided with portable religious literature of a somewhat startling character, and was in this way able to supply his fellow-passengers in the evening 'bus; and it was stimulating to any one with a sense of humour to see commercial magnates handling one of Elijah's tracts as if it were dynamite, and late-comers taking in the interior at a glance from the step, and hurriedly climbing to the top—willing to risk bronchitis rather than twenty minutes of Elijah. His conscientious opinion was that the limited number of persons who held his particular opinions would go to heaven, and the large number who did not would go elsewhere, and in these circumstances no one could blame him for being urgent. No doubt Elijah—for indeed this was almost an official title—was very insistent, and had no tact; but then when you are pulling people out of fires, and handing them out of burning houses—these were his favourite illustrations of the situation—one does not pay much attention to ceremony or even manners. It was often said that he alienated people from religion, and so defeated his own ends; but I suppose that his reply would be that he left them no worse than he found them, and if it was asserted that he influenced no one, he very likely had some cases of success among that class of persons who are never utterly persuaded until they are felled by a blow between the eyes. Very likely he was not concerned about success or failure, approval or disapproval, but simply was determined to do his duty, which was to hold back as many of his neighbours as he could from going to Hell. This duty he discharged with all his might and with undeniable courage, and Elijah had his reward by universal consent in that no one accused him of canting, for he never said anything he did not believe with the marrow of his bones, or of hypocrisy, for he certainly made no gain of godliness.

When Elijah entered my room one morning—his clean-shaven, heavy-jawed face more determined than ever—I was certain that he had not come to talk over the weather, and prepared myself for faithful dealing.

"It is not my custom," he began, "to read fiction, and I believe that the more people read novels the less will they want to read their Bibles; but I was recommended to read a book of yours, called *The Days of Auld Lang Syne*, by a friend, in whose judgment I have usually placed confidence, and I feel it my duty to call and remonstrate with you about that book."

Was it the literary form that he wished to criticise, or the substance? In either case I hoped he would speak with all frankness, an encouragement which Mr. Higginbotham perhaps hardly needed.

"Well, I don't know anything about literature, for I thank God that my Bible and the *Pilgrim's Progress* are enough for me; but I did once read Scott—long ago before I knew the value of time—and your book is certainly not up to that sample."

This, I assured Elijah, was my own fixed and unalterable opinion, and I ventured to congratulate Elijah on the acuteness of his literary judgment—which compliment was passed over without acknowledgment—and then I pressed for his farther criticism.

"What I have to say is just this, that there are characters in the book who ought not to be introduced to a Christian family, and views which are sure to injure religion."

Now it happened that I had been reading that morning an interesting and very caustic review, in which it was pointed out that no people had ever lived or ever would live so good as the inhabitants of Drumtochty: that I had confused together the (mythical) garden of Eden with a Scots village; that the places were really very different in morals and general environment; that it was a pity that the author did not know the limits of true art; that what was wanted was reality, not sentimental twaddle, and that in short—but this is not how the critic put it—let the writer of fiction stick to the ash-pit in a house, and not attempt the picture gallery. The critic—a young gentleman, I should say—was very severe on my London doctor, who had taken a servant girl to his own house that she might die there in peace, and assured me that such extravagant unrealities showed my hopeless ignorance, and proved my unfitness to be an artist in life. Up to this point I had been much humbled, and had been trying to profit by every word of wisdom; but now I laid down the paper and had a few moments of sinless enjoyment, for this incident had been lifted bodily out of life, with only some change in names, and was the only fact in the book. A poor puling idealist!—yet even in my most foolish flights I had kept some hold on life—but here was Elijah Higginbotham sitting calmly in my study and suggesting that I was a realist of such a pronounced and shameless character that my books were not fit for family reading.

When I pressed him for some evidence of his charge, he cited "Posty," and spoke briefly but strongly about that unfortunate man's taste for alcoholic liquors.

"Could I reconcile it with my conscience to introduce such a man to the Christian public, and was I not aware of the injury which drink was doing in our country?"

"Mr. Higginbotham," I said, "my business was to represent life in a Scots parish, within limits, as I had seen it, and although I say it with deep regret, and hope the matter will never be mentioned outside this room, every Scot is not a rigid and bigoted abstainer—a few, I hope fewer every year, do 'taste.'"

"We are all perfectly aware of that, and more than a few,"—which was not generous on his part,—"but that is not the question. It is whether you as a respectable—and I would fain believe in spite of what I have read—Christian man, ought deliberately to condone and countenance this conduct."

"Surely, sir, you do not suppose for one moment that I have the slightest sympathy with intemperance, or that I did not deeply regret the habits into which Posty had fallen! Had I known that you or any intelligent person would have imagined such a thing, I would have added footnotes, whenever Posty forgot himself, such as (1) The author deeply regrets Posty's conduct; (2) The author repudiates Posty's language with all his heart."

"It might have saved misunderstanding." Elijah regarded me dubiously. "I would certainly not have judged that you felt so strongly from the book."

"Ah, there you are wrong, for again and again I simply wrestled with Posty to take the blue ribbon; but you know one should not boast, and it would have sounded egotistical to obtrude these efforts, unhappily unsuccessful, in the book.

"It is," I ventured to add with some pathos, "very hard that I should first of all have had to suffer from my association, even in a literary sense, with Posty, and then afterwards to be treated by religious and philanthropic persons as if I had been his boon companion."

"No, no; don't put words in my mouth," broke in Elijah. "I said nothing of the kind; but you have not been careful to convey your own position,"

AN EVANGELIST

"Mr. Higginbotham, if I might give you a word of advice, do not meddle with fiction, for you never can tell into what company you may come. Why, I may tell you that 'Posty,' before his lamented death, used to haunt this room—in a literary sense, of course—and some evenings I was terrified.

"If he were (comparatively) sober he would confine himself to the news of the district, and the subject of her Majesty's mails; but if he had been tasting he always took to theology, as Scots generally do, and then he grew so profound and eloquent on the doctrine of election that if you had come in my character would have been worth nothing: you would have jumped to the conclusion, not without reason, that he had got his refreshments here."

"You will excuse me," said Elijah, who had lost his customary expression of cocksureness during the last few minutes, "I am out of touch with the market: am I not right in understanding that the Postman was never alive?"

"Well, I'm sorry you have thought so, for it would be rather a severe reflection on his author; but I think he must have had some life, else you would not have done him (and me) the honour of so much attention."

"He was your manufacture or creation, in fact done for the book; put it as you please—you know what I mean"—and my visitor grew impatient.

"Then, if that be so, you could make him say and do what you pleased."

"In fact, take the blue ribbon and become an example for temperance speeches."

"Why not?" replied Elijah stoutly; "it might have done good."

"Mr. Higginbotham," I said with much solemnity, "be thankful that in your busy and blameless life you have never meddled with fiction, save, I fancy, in commercial transactions; for you have escaped trials of anxiety and disappointment beyond anything in the markets. You suppose, I notice, that because a story-teller creates certain characters, he can do with them as he pleases, putting words into their mouths and dictating their marriages."

"Well, naturally I do."

"Nothing of the kind, sir. Once these characters are fairly started on their career, and come of age, as it were, they go their own way, and the whole of their author's time is taken up following them, remonstrating with them, and trying, generally in vain, to get them to work out his plan. Now you would say, I fancy, that the poor author could at least settle their marriages."

"I would do so," said Elijah grimly, "if I were writing."

"Unfortunately that is one of the most difficult and delicate parts of a poor novelist's work, and he fails as often as he succeeds. The man marries the wrong woman, and *vice versâ*, till the author is

AN EVANGELIST

in despair, and sometimes wishes he had never called such a set of rebels into existence."

Elijah looked incredulous.

"I can assure you, you never know what secret they may have in their past lives, or what love affairs are going on behind your back. I'll give you an illustration, if I may quote from very simple fiction. A lady wrote me, after the publication of the *Brier Bush*, that she believed Drumsheugh was in love with Marget Howe, and wished to know whether this was the case? I replied that this suspicion had crossed my own mind, and that I was watching events. And as you have done me the honour of reading *Auld Lang Syne*, you will remember that Drumsheugh had been a faithful, although undeclared lover of Marget since early manhood. Yet it came on me as a surprise; and if any one had said, Why did not you tell this sooner? my answer would have been, I did not know. If I am not wearying you, Mr. Higginbotham—I am on my defence, and I should like to have your good opinion—I may confess that I tried to arrange, in a book, a girl's love affairs, and she married the wrong man, one quite unsuited for her, and the result was—although this is again a secret—they have had many unnecessary trials. No, no, we are helpless creatures, we so-called authors; poor mother hens, beseeching from the edge of the pond and lamenting, while the brood of ducklings swim away in all directions."

"That's all very well; and, as writing is not in

my line, you may be right; but I have not come to my most serious ground of complaint, and that is the Postman's—er—judgment and future lot."

"Yes," I said, and waited for the indictment.

"Here, according to your own description, is a man"—and Elijah checked off the list of my poor gossip's sins on his fingers—"who makes no profession of religion—vital religion, I mean, for theology is a mere matter of the head—who indulged in spirituous liquors to excess, who refused tracts, when they were offered, with contempt, who to all appearance had never known any saving change. He dies suddenly, and bravely, I admit, but with no sign of repentance, and this man, dying in his sin, is sent to Heaven as if he were a saint. If that is what happened with the Postman," summed up Elijah with uncompromising decision, "then I do not know the Gospel. 'He that believeth shall be saved, and he that believeth not shall be damned,' is plain enough. He wasn't saved here—no one could say that. 'As the tree falleth, so shall it lie.' He couldn't be saved there. Yes, it may sound severe, but it is the truth, and there is no room for sentiment in religion; your story is grossly misleading, and may do injury to many precious souls."

"By moving people, do you mean, to give their lives for others and to forget themselves?" I dared to ask.

"I don't deny that it was a gallant deed to jump into the river and save the girl's life," replied Elijah

AN EVANGELIST

hastily. "I appreciate that; but it's not by works that any one can be saved. What right had you to send that man to Heaven?"

"Mr. Higginbotham, you are still making me the scapegoat for other men's acts. I was only the historian. It was Jamie Soutar and Carmichael, the Free Kirk minister, who held a council on the road one day, and decided that it must be well with Posty because he died to save a little child. Jamie has always been a trial to me, and a ground of criticism, especially because he used to cloak his good deeds with falsehood to escape praise instead of proclaiming them at the corners of the streets as the good people used to do. So little sympathy have I with Jamie, that before the proof sheets of the book left this room I sent for Jamie (in a literary sense), and he came (in the same sense), and I placed him just where you are sitting and spoke to him (always in the same sense) very seriously. May I tell you—as it will further vindicate me—what I said?

"Thank you, sir, for your patience. 'James,' I said—for if any one is usually called Jamie and on some occasion you say James, it is very impressive —'if these sheets are printed as they stand, I'm afraid both you and I will suffer at the hands of the good people, and, with your permission, there is one passage at least I would like to amend.'

"'What is it?' said Jamie quickly, but, I felt, unresponsively.

"'It's where you go up to London solely to visit the poor servant lass, and then say you are in charge of Drumsheugh's cattle; where you assure Lily that her mistress had been enquiring for her, when you had just rated her mistress for cruel carelessness; where you give Lily twenty pounds as from her mistress, while it is your own money: all to cheer a poor dying lassie, James, I admit, but not true, not true.'

"'What wud ye hev me to say?' enquired Jamie, but very drily indeed.

"'Well, I have written a sentence or two, James, which I hope you will allow me to insert, and I am sure our critics will be quite satisfied; it's what they would say themselves.'

"'Read on,' said Jamie, looking very hard.

"'Here I am, Lily, a' the way frae Drumtochty, ane's errand to see ye—a matter o' five pounds outlay, I reckon, but what's that 'atween friends? And here's twenty punds o' ma hard-earned savin's a've brocht ye; ye'll pay me back gin ye be spared; an' gin things come to the worst, yir grandmother's honest; interest needna be mentioned unless ye insist, and ye maunna tell onybody what a've done for ye, except a friend or two in the Glen.'

"'Are ye prood o' that passage?' enquired Jamie, and his tone was distinctly disagreeable; 'd'ye think it a credit to you or me?'

"'It's safe, James, and will be acceptable.'

"Mr. Higginbotham, you will have some idea

AN EVANGELIST 259

what sort of men I've had to deal with, and will be more merciful to me when I tell you that Jamie walked to the door without a word and then gave me his answer: 'Ye hev ae Pharisee in yer book; an' gin ye want two, a'm no the man.' You can see yourself what a man of Jamie Soutar's peculiar disposition would do, if he had the power, with poor Posty, who gave his life for a little maid."

"More than Jamie Soutar would . . . in fact, let Posty off"—Elijah spoke with some feeling—" and it's a mercy that such decisions are not in our hands. We must just go by Revelation, and I do not see any way of escape. As regards Jamie, I cannot approve of deliberate falsehood, and I wish to say so distinctly, but I understand and . . . appreciate his motive."

As Elijah said this, certain stories came suddenly into my mind: how he would have a hot altercation with some man on religion, but afterwards would do him a good turn in business; how a young fellow had insulted him in a 'bus, and in a great strait, had been helped by some unknown person, and he always believed himself that the person was Elijah. It seemed to me as if the evangelist's face had relaxed a little, and that beneath this casing of doctrine a heart might be beating. So I went on with my defence.

"The other judge who took upon him to reward 'Posty' in the next world was the Free Kirk minister, and I always regarded Carmichael as a heady young man, too much inclined to take up with new views, and not sufficiently respectful to the past. But young men have generous impulses, and I suppose Carmichael's heart got the better of his head as he thought of Posty giving all he had—his life— for the drowning lassie."

"He would have been unworthy the name of a man, let alone a minister," broke in Elijah, "if he had not admired that deed. Do you think I don't . . . appreciate the devotion of such a man? It was admirable, and Mr. Carmichael is to be excused if he . . . did go too far."

So Elijah really was the "Produce Broker" who headed the subscription for the widows and orphans of the gallant lifeboats-men. Some had laughed the idea to scorn, saying that he would never give £100 to any object except tracts or missions. They did not know my evangelist. Whatever he compelled himself to think the Almighty would do with men, Posty had been very well off indeed with Elijah as judge.

"Mr. Higginbotham," I said, taking a rapid resolution, "it does not matter what I think, for a humble story-teller is no theologian, and it matters as little what my friends of the book thought: let me tell the story over again in brief, and I shall leave you to pronounce 'Posty's' doom."

"It's far later than I supposed," and Elijah rose hastily, "and I'm afraid I must go: the market is very sensitive at present. Some other day we can talk the matter over. I have no wish to be uncharitable, whatever people may think of me, but we must obey the truth. Well, if you insist—just ten minutes. . . . It is not by our feelings, however, that such things are to be decided." Elijah sat down again, looking just a shade too stern, as if he were afraid of his own integrity, and not perfectly sure that the Bible would back him.

"It was Mrs. Macfadyen's youngest daughter, you remember, who fell into the Tochty, and Elsie was everybody's favourite. She was a healthy and winsome child, with fair hair and bright laughing eyes. . . ."

"Blue?" suddenly enquired Elijah, and then added in some confusion, "I beg your pardon; I was thinking of a child I once knew, and . . . loved. Go on."

"Yes, blue, about the colour of a forget-me-not. . . ."

"Hers were darker, like the sea, you know, and in her last illness they were as deep . . . I interrupt you."

"People liked Elsie because she was such a merry soul: coming to meet you on the road, nodding to you over a hedge, or giving you a kiss if you wished."

. Elijah nodded as one who understood; yet he was a wifeless, childless man. Some child friendship most likely; and now, even as I glance at him from the corner of my eyes, his friend is putting her arms round his neck. Would they recognise him in the 'bus at this moment?

"Her mother was washing blankets by the edge of the river, which was in flood, and rising, and the lassie was playing beside her with a doll. She was singing at the very time in gladness of heart and thinking of no danger."

"Poor little woman!" It gave one a start, for this was a new voice, unknown in the lard market or the religious meeting. What had become of Elijah Higginbotham?

"When she either stooped too near the flood, or a larger wave had caught her where she sat, and at the sound of a scream her mother looked round, and saw the wee lassie disappear in the black cauldron which whirled round and round within the rocks."

"Ah!" groaned Elijah, visibly moved, who had spoken calmly of the everlasting damnation of the greater portion of the human race times without number.

"Her mother, in her agony, cried to God to save Elsie."

"She could not have done better," cried Elijah; "and He answered her prayer."

"While she prayed, Posty was coming down the footpath behind, and he heard her cry."

"Posty was the instrument," and Elijah rapped the floor with his stick. "He obeyed the Divine command within, and he cannot go without some reward."

"He tore off his coat in an instant, and then—I suppose if you had been there you would have besought him to bethink himself: and to remember that he was a man unfit to die! Is not that so?"

"Sir," said Elijah, "you do me less than justice, and . . . insult me. What right have you to ask me such a question? I have preached, and I will preach again; but there's a time for preaching, and a time to refrain from preaching. I can swim, and I have saved two lives in my time. I am a fool for boasting, but I would . . ."

"I believe you would, Mr. Higginbotham"—I saw an able-bodied man without fear—"and I beg your pardon . . ."

Elijah waved his hand. I was to go on to the end without delay.

"It seemed fifteen minutes, it was only one, while the mother hung over the edge of the black seething whirlpool, and then he came up, bleeding from a wound in the forehead, without Elsie."

"I take you to witness," declared Elijah solemnly, "that I said he was a brave man. Yes, he had the natural virtues, and some who make a profession have none."

"For a few seconds he hung on to the edge to get breath, and Mrs. Macfadyen herself besought him not to risk his life, for he was a husband and father; but he only answered: 'I'll hae Elsie oot,'"

"They forgot themselves,—do you mark that?—both of them," cried Elijah. "Whose spirit was that? Didn't they keep the commandment of Love, which is the chief commandment? and—answer me—can any one keep that commandment without grace?"

It was not with me but with himself the evangelist was arguing, and I went on:

"He came up again, this time with Elsie in one arm, a poor, little limp bundle of clothes, her yellow hair spread over her face, and her eyes closed, I was afraid, for ever."

"But she lived, didn't she?" There was no Elijah Higginbotham anywhere to be found now, only an excited man, concerned about the saving of a little maid. "Excuse me, I didn't read that part about the saving so carefully as I ought. I was more concerned about . . . the judgment."

"Yes, Elsie was all right in a day or two, but Posty had not strength to do more than hand her to her mother, and then, exhausted by the struggle with the water, he fell back, and was dead when he was found."

"What were you doing that you did not lay hold of Posty and pull him out?" thundered Elijah; "you seem to have been there."

"Only in a literary sense," I hastened to explain, for it now seemed likely that the evangelist, having come to condemn Posty, was about to take up the cudgels on his behalf.

AN EVANGELIST

"I wish to Heaven you had been there in a physical sense; you would have been far more useful!" replied Elijah. "And so he died and Elsie was saved?"

"Yes, Posty died and went to his account; that was how he lived, and that was how he died." And I waited.

Elijah sprang out of his seat and stood on the hearthrug, his face flushed, and his eyes shining.

"It's a pity that he tasted; I wish he hadn't. It's a pity he did not think more about his own soul; I wish he had. But Posty was a hero, and played the man that day. Posty will have another chance. Posty loved, and God is Love; if there's such a thing as justice, it's all right with Posty."

We did not look at one another for a full minute—a print of Perugino's Crucifixion over the mantelpiece interested me, and Elijah's eye seemed to be arrested by the *Encyclopaedia Britannica* on the other side of the room—a minute later we shook hands upon the basis of the Divine Love and our humanity, and nothing more passed between us.

From my window I could see him go along the street. He stopped and slapped his leg triumphantly. I seemed to hear the evangelist say again with great joy: "It's all right with Posty!" I said, "And it's all right with Elijah Higginbotham."

THE COLLECTOR'S INCON-
SISTENCY

THE COLLECTOR'S INCON-
SISTENCY

There were many capable men in the session of the North Free Kirk, Muirtown—such as Bailie MacCallum, from whom Drumsheugh bought Kate Carnegie's wedding present after a historical tussle—but they were all as nothing beside the Collector, and this was so well known in Muirtown that people spoke freely of the Collector's kirk. When he arrived in Muirtown, it was understood that he sampled six kirks, three Established and three Free—the rumour about the Original Seceders was never authenticated—and that the importance of his visits was thoroughly appreciated. No unseemly fuss was made on his appearance; but an ex-bailie, or the Clerk to the Road Trustees, or some such official person, happened to meet him at the door, and received him into his pew with quiet, unostentatious respect; and when he left, officious deacons did not encompass his exit, rubbing their hands and asking how he liked their place, but an elder journeying in the same direction entered into general conversation and was able to mention with authority next day what the Collector had said. Various reasons were canvassed for his settlement in the North Kirk, where old Dr. Pittendriegh was then drawing near to the close of his famous exposition of the Epistle to the Romans, published after the Doctor's death, and sold to the extent of fifty-seven copies among the congregation. It was, for one thing, a happy coincidence that on that occasion the Doctor, having taken an off day from Romans, had preached from the text "Render unto Cæsar the things which are Cæsar's," and had paid a high tribute to the character of a faithful servant of the Crown. Some importance, no doubt, also attached to the fact that the Procurator Fiscal sat in the "North Free," austere and mysterious, whose power of detecting crime bordered on the miraculous, and whose ways were veiled in impenetrable darkness, so that any one with a past felt uncomfortable in his presence; and it was almost synonymous with doom to say of a man, "The Fiscal has his eye on him." Perhaps it was not without influence that the Supervisor, who was the Collector's subordinate, with power also of official life and death, had long sat under Dr. Pittendriegh—the Doctor and the Collector were indeed the only persons the Supervisor did sit under. He had admirable opportunities of enlarging to the Collector on the solid and edifying qualities of Dr. Pittendriegh's ministry, and the unfortunate defects in the preaching and pastoral gifts of neighbouring ministers, in the intervals of business, when the

INCONSISTENCY

two of them were not investigating into the delinquencies of some officer of excise, who had levied a tax on the produce of Dunleith Distillery not only in money but also in kind; or concocting cunning plans for the detection of certain shepherds who were supposed to be running an entirely unlicensed still in the recesses of Glen Urtach. It was at least through this official, himself an elder, that the Collector's decision was intimated to the Doctor and the other authorities of the North Kirk, and they lost no time in giving it proper and irrevocable effect. The Supervisor set an example of patriotic sacrifice by surrendering his pew in the centre of the church and retiring to the modest obscurity of the side seats so that the Collector could be properly housed; for it was not to be thought of for a moment that he should sit anywhere except in the eye of the public, or that ordinary persons—imagine for instance young children—should be put in the same pew with him. So he sat there alone, for he had neither wife nor child, from January to December, except when on his official leave—which he took not for pleasure but from a sense of duty—and he gave a calm, judicial attention to all the statements put before him by the preacher. Very soon after this arrangement the Doctor discovered that the Deacons' Court required strengthening, and, as a man of affairs, the Collector was added at the head of the list; and when a year later a happy necessity compelled an election of elders, the Collector was raised to this higher degree, and thereafter was "thirled" to the North Free, and the history of that kirk and of the Collector became one.

What exactly the great man collected, or what functions and powers might be included in his office, were not matters Muirtown pretended to define or dared to pry into. It was enough that he was, in the highest and final sense of the word, Collector—no mere petty official of a local body, but the representative of the Imperial Government and the commissioned servant of Her Majesty the Queen, raised above principalities and powers in the shape of bailies and provosts, and owning no authority save, as was supposed, the Chancellor of the Exchequer. For any one to confound him with the collector of, say, water rates was either abysmal ignorance or, it might be, although one hoped not, a piece of Radical insolence and a despising of dignities. It was good manners to call him by his title—many would have had difficulty in mentioning his private name, which was, I believe, Thomas Richard Thorne, just as the Queen's, I believe, is Guelph—and it was pleasing to hear a porter at the station shout, amid a crowd of tourists going to the Kilspindie Arms, "Collector's cab"; or Bailie MacCallum on the street, "Fine morning, Collector"; and one did not wonder that the session of the "North Free" exalted its head when this kind of thing went on at its meetings: " Moderator, with your permission, I would like to have the mind of the Collector "; and then in reply, " Moderator, my views practically coincide with those of the Fiscal." And there were dinner tables, such as old Peter MacCash's, the manager of the Muirtown Bank, where conversation reached a very high level of decoration, and nothing could be heard save " Sheriff," " Provost," " Collector," " Town Clerk," " Fiscal," " Banker," " Doctor," " Dean of Guild," and such like, till an untitled person hardly dared to defend his most cherished opinion.

As the movements of Government officials were always mysterious, no one could tell whence the Collector had come, but it was known to a few that he was not really of Scots blood, and had not been bred in the Presbyterian Kirk. When his hand in the way of Church rule was heavy on the " North Free " and certain sought anxiously for grounds of revolt, they were apt to whisper that, after all, this man, who laid down the ecclesiastical law with such pedantic accuracy and such inflexible severity, was but a gentile who had established himself in the true fold, or at most a proselyte of the gate. They even dared to ask what, in the matter of churches, he had been before he was appointed to Muirtown; and so unscrupulous and virulent are the mongers of sedition, as every student of history knows, that some insinuated that the Collector had been a Nonconformist; while others, considering that this violence could only overreach itself, contented themselves with allusions to Swedenborg. Most of his brethren treated him as if he had been within the covenant from the beginning, and had been granted the responsible privilege of Scots birth either because in course of time they had forgotten the fact of alien origin in face of every appearance to the contrary, or because, as we all need mercy, it is not wise to search too curiously into the dark chapters of a man's past.

Upon his part the Collector had wonderfully adapted himself to the new environment, and it defied the keenest critic to find in him any trace of a former home. It is true that he did not use the Scots dialect, merely employing a peculiarly felicitous word at a time for purposes of effect, but he had stretched his vowels to the orthodox breadth, and could roll off the letter " r " with a sense of power. " Dour " he could say in a way that deceived even the elect. Sometimes he startled the Presbytery with a sound like " Yah, yah," which indicates the shallow sharpness of the English, instead of " He-e-er, he-e-er," which reveals as in a symbol the solidity of the Scot; but then one cannot live in London for years—as an official must—and be quite unscathed; and an acute observer might mark a subdued smartness in dress—white tie instead of stock on sacrament

Sabbaths—which was not indigenous; but then it must be allowed that one in his position was obliged to be, to a certain degree, a man of the world. No one ever caught him quoting a clause from the Prayer-Book on the rare occasions when he was heard at his family devotions, or breaking into a riotous "Hallelujah" in the midst of a sermon. If misfortune had thrown him into Episcopalian or Methodist folds in earlier years, he had since been thoroughly purged and cleansed. He had a way of alluding to "the Disruption principles laid down in 1843," or "my younger brethren will allow me to say that the Disruption," which was very convincing; and on the solitary occasion when he made a set speech in public—for his strength lay in silence rather than eloquence—he had a peroration on our "covenanted forefathers" which left an indelible impression. It was understood that he spent his holidays in visiting remote districts of the Highlands where the people took strong peppermints in church without scruple or apology, and preserved the primeval simplicity of Presbyterian worship entire; and it was supposed that he was looking for a birthplace which would finally establish his position as an elder of the Kirk.

What gave the Collector his supreme influence in the session of the Free North, and extended his sphere of ecclesiastical influence to the Presbytery of Muirtown, was an amazing knowledge of Church law and a devouring love for order.

The latter may have been the natural outcome of his professional training, wherein red-tape has been raised to a science, but the former was an acquired accomplishment. Dr. Pittendriegh remembered almost painfully that on the day of his election to the eldership the Collector enquired the names of the most reliable authorities on Church law, and that he (Dr. Pittendriegh) had not only given him a list, but had urged him to their study, judging from past experience that no man was likely to go too far in the pursuit of this branch of knowledge. For a while the Collector sat silent and observant at the meetings of Session, and then suddenly one evening, and in the quietest manner, he inquired whether a certain proceeding was in order.

"Well, at any rate, that is how we have done here for twenty years," said the Doctor, with just a flavour of indignation, and the startled Fiscal confirmed the statement.

"That may be so, Moderator, and I am obliged to Mr. Fiscal for his assurance, but you will pardon me for saying, with much respect, that the point is not whether this action has been the custom, but whether it is legal. On that, Moderator, I should like your deliverance."

He took the opportunity, however, of showing that only one deliverance could be given by long quotations from Church law, supported by references which extended back to the seventeenth century. Every one knew that, unlike his distinguished colleague in Muirtown Dr. Dowbiggin, the minister of the Free North was more at home in Romans than in Canon Law; but, like every true Scot, he loved a legal point, and he not only announced at next Session meeting that the Collector was quite right, but expressed his satisfaction that they had such a valuable addition to their number in the Collector. His position from that evening was assured beyond dispute; and when the Clerk of Session resigned on the ground of long service, but really through terror that there might be a weak place in his minutes, the Collector succeeded, and made the proceedings of the Free North Session to be a wonder unto many. It was a disappointment to some that, when the Collector was sent to the Presbytery, he took no part for several meetings; but others boldly declared that even in that high place he was only biding his time, which came when the Presbytery debated for one hour and ten minutes whether a certain meeting had been *pro re nata*, or *in hunc effectum*, while the learned clerk listened with delight as one watches the young people at play.

"Moderator," said the Collector, "I have given the most careful attention to the arguments on both sides, and I venture to suggest that the meeting was neither *pro re nata* nor *in hunc effectum*, but was a meeting *per saltum*"; and, after referring to Pardovan's Institutes, he sat down amid a silence which might be felt. Several ministers openly confessed their ignorance one to another with manifest chagrin, and one young minister laughed aloud: "*Per saltum*, I declare—what next?" as if it were a subject for jesting.

"The Collector is quite right, Moderator," said the Clerk with his unspeakable air of authority; "the meeting referred to was undoubtedly *per saltum*, but I did not wish to interfere prematurely with the debate"; and from that date the Clerk, who used to address his more recondite deliverances to Dr. Dowbiggin as the only competent audience, was careful to include the Collector in a very marked and flattering fashion.

While it was only human that his congregation should be proud of the Collector, and while there is no question that he led them in the paths of order, they sometimes grumbled—in corners—and grew impatient under his rule. He was not only not a man given to change himself, but he bitterly resented and resisted to the uttermost any proposal of change on the part of other people. What was in the Free North, when he, so to say, mounted the throne, was right, and any departure therefrom he scented afar off and opposed as folly and mischief. There are men whom you can convince by argument; there are others whom you can talk round on trifles; but whether the matter were great or small—from Biblical criticism, on which the Collector took a liberal line, to the printing of the congregational report, where he would not allow a change of type—once his mind was made up he remained unchangeable and inaccessible. He prevented the introduction of hymns for ten years, and never consented to the innovation on the ground of the hold which the metrical psalms had upon Presbyterians from their earliest days, and he did succeed in retaining that remarkable custom of the Scots Kirk by which a communicant cannot receive the Sacrament without first presenting a leaden token, and his argument was again the sacred associations of the past. He did certainly agree to the recovering of the pulpit cushions, which the exposition of Romans had worn bare, only, however, on the assurance of Bailie MacCallum, given officially, that he had the same cloth in store; but a scheme for a ventilating chamber in the roof—an improvement greatly needed in a church which was supposed to have retained the very air of the Disruption—he denounced as an irresponsible fad.

He gave much watchful attention to the Sabbath schools—"Sunday" was a word he abhorred—and between the Collector and the younger people engaged in that work there was almost constant conflict, which extended to every detail, and came to a head over the matter of entertainments. It was their belief that once a year it was necessary for the success and well-being of a Sabbath school that the children should be gathered on an evening and fed with tea and buns, and afterwards elevated by magic slides representing various amusing situations in life and concluding with a vivid picture of rats disappearing into a gaping man's mouth, which opened to receive them with a jerk. The fact that this festivity was opened and closed with a hymn in no way sanctified it in the eyes of the Collector, who declared it to be without any Scripture warrant and injurious to true religion, as well as—and this was hardly less important—quite without sanction by the laws of the Kirk. By sheer force of will—the weight of a silent, obstinate uncompromising nature, he brought the "treats"—very modest, innocent, if not particularly refined efforts to give some brightness to the life of the poor children in Muirtown—to an end, and in place thereof he provided, at his own expense, views of the mission stations of the world, with a gratuitous distribution of missionary literature. This was endured for three years with much discontent and with sudden and disorderly demands for the rats in place of the interesting although somewhat monotonous faces of Chinese Christians, and then the rebellion was organized which had so unexpected and felicitous a result.

The party of the juniors, some of them approaching forty years of age, took a covenant that they would stand by one another, and they made their plan that upon a certain evening in March they would gather together their corps of Muirtown Arabs and feed them with dainties even unto

INCONSISTENCY

the extent of raisins and oranges. They were not unconscious that oranges, on account of their pronounced colour, would be an offence to the Collector, and that that estimable man had already referred to this fruit, as a refreshment at a religious meeting, in terms of deep contempt; and there would not only be a magic lantern with scenes of war and sport, to say nothing of amusement, but also a sacred cantata to be sung by the children. When the Collector heard of the programme, he grasped the situation at once, and knew that in the coming battle quarter could not be given—that the " Reds " would be completely reduced to subordination, or that a severely constitutional monarchy would be finally closed. This was indeed the general opinion; and when the Juniors appeared before the Session to present their ultimatum, nothing but a sense of decency prevented the Free North attending in a body, and Bailie MacCallum took a gloomy view of the issue.

" Oranges and the what-ye-call-it," alluding to the Cantata, " the Collector 'll never stand, and ye couldna expect him."

Dr. Pittendriegh was now *emeritus*, which means that he had retired from the active duty of the ministry and was engaged in criticising those who were still in the yoke; and many pitied young Mr. Rutherford, brother of Rutherford of Glasgow, who had to preside over so critical a meeting. His prayer was, however, favourably received by both sides, and his few remarks before calling on the leader of the " Reds " were full of tact and peace. As for that intrepid man—grocer by trade and full of affability, but a Radical in politics and indifferent to the past—he discharged a difficult duty, with considerable ability. For himself and his friends he disclaimed all desire to offend any one, and least of all one whom every one respected so much for his services both to Church and State—both the Bailie and Fiscal felt bound to say " hear, hear," and the Collector bowed stiffly—but they must put the work they had carried on in the Vennel before any individual; they were dealing with a poor and neglected class of children very different from the children in grand houses—this with some teethiness. They must make religion attractive, and show that they were interested in the children's lives as well as their souls. None of them could see anything wrong in a cup of tea or a bit of music; and if the Session was to forbid this small pleasure, he and his friends would respectfully resign the position they had held for many years, and allow the elders to carry on the work on any plan they pleased.

There was a faint rustle; the Bailie gave a low whistle, and then the Collector rose from the table, where he sat as clerk, removed the gold eyeglass from his nose with much deliberation, coughed slightly, and waving his eyeglass gently with his left hand, gave his deliverance. He acknowledged with somewhat cold courtesy the generous expressions regarding any slight services he had been allowed to render in his dual capacity, and he desired to express his profound sense of the devotion with which his friends on the other side, if he might just for the occasion speak of sides, carried on their important work. His difficulty, however, was this—and he feared that it was insuperable—Christian work must be carried on in accordance with sound principles, by the example of the Bible and according to the spirit of the Scots Kirk. He was convinced that the entertainments in question, with the accompaniments to which he would not further allude in this place, were quite contrary to the sound and solid traditions which were very dear to some of them, and from which he ventured to hope the Free North Church of Muirtown would never depart. If the Session should take another view than that of his humble judgment, then nothing would remain for him but to resign his position as Session Clerk and Elder. There was general consternation on the faces of his brethren, and even the Juniors looked uncomfortable, and the Moderator did wisely in adjourning the meeting for a week.

The idea was some kind of compromise; but no one was particularly hopeful, and the first essays were not very encouraging. It was laid on the Bailie to deal with the leader of the insurgents, for the sound reason that, as every class has its own freemasonry, one tradesman was likely to know how to deal with another. No man had a more plausible tongue, as was well known in municipal circles, and the Bailie plied the grocer with the arguments of expediency: that the Collector was an ornament to the Free North; that any disruption in their congregation would be a sport to the Philistines; that if you offended the Collector, you touched the Fiscal and the other professional dignitaries; that it would be possible to go a good way in the direction that the insurgents desired without attracting any notice; and that the Collector. . . . " Well, ye see, Councillor "—for the grocer had so far attained—" there's bound to be changes; we maun be prepared for that. He's failin' a wee, an' there's nae use counterin' him." So, with many shrugs and suggestions, the astute politician advised that the insurgents should make a nominal submission and wait their time. Then the Councillor informed the Bailie that he would fight the battle to the end, although the Collector should join the Established Kirk, and Bailie MacCallum knew that his labour had been all in vain.

It was the Fiscal who approached the Collector, as was most meet, and he considered that the best time was after dinner, and when the two were discussing their second glass of port.

"That's a sound wine, Collector, and a credit to a Muirtown firm. Remarkable man, old Sandeman; established a good port in Scotland and invented a new denomination, when to save my life I couldn't have thought of another."

"So far as I can judge, I do not think that Sandemanianism is any credit to Muirtown. How any Scots Kirkman can sink down into that kind of thing passes me. But the wine is unexceptionable, and I never tasted any but good wine at your table; yet I suppose young men would prefer claret —not the rich claret Scots gentlemen used to drink, but that feeble Gladstone stuff," and the Collector wagged his head in sorrow over the decadent taste of the day.

"I quite agree with you, Collector, but you know *de gustibus;* and when the young fellows do me the honour of dining with me, I let them have their claret: there must be give and take between the seniors and juniors, eh, Collector?"—this with some adroitness.

"There I venture to disagree with you, Fiscal," and the Collector's face hardened at once. "It is the young who ought to yield to the old; I see no reason why the old should give in to the young; if they do, the end will be anarchy in Church and State."

"There is a great deal in what you say, Collector, but have you never been afraid that if we of the old school refuse to make any concessions, we shall simply lose our influence, and things will be done foolishly, which, with our help, might have been done wisely?"

"If there be one word I detest, it is 'concessions'; they are ruinous, both in the Civil Service and in the Church; and it just comes to this, Fiscal: if you yield an inch, you must yield a yard. Nothing will preserve order save resistance from the beginning, *obsta principiis*, yes, *obsta principiis*."

The Fiscal recognised the expression on the Collector's face, and knew that it was useless to continue the subject, and so his labour was also in vain.

It only now remained that the minister should try his hand upon this inflexible man, and one of the urgent duties of his pastoral office hindered him until the evening before the meeting. During the last few days Rutherford had been trying to get the key to this type of character, and had been touched by the Collector's loneliness. Without wife or child, engaged in routine year by year, moving in a narrow set of officials or ecclesiastics, he had withered and contracted till he had become a mere pedant. People spoke of his narrowness and obstinacy. They were angry with him, and would not be sorry to teach him a lesson. The minister's heart was full of pity and charity; and, so optimistic is youth, he believed that there must be springs of emotion and romance in the old man; but this faith he did not mention to the Bailie or the Fiscal, considering, with some reason, that they would put it down as a foolish dream, and be inwardly much amused. As he stood before the Collector's residence, as it was called in the *Muirtown Advertiser,* his pity deepened, and he seemed to be confirmed in his compassion. The Collector did not live in rooms or in a small house as did other bachelors, for this would be unworthy of his position, and a reflection on the State; but he must needs live in a house on the North Meadow. The large drawing-room lay unused and empty, since no ladies came to the house; and of the bedrooms only three were furnished: one for his servants, one for himself, and another a guest-room, which was never occupied save by some Government official from London on inspection, or a minister attending the Presbytery. The Collector was eager to secure Rabbi Saunderson, but that learned man, of absent mind, was apt to forget that he had been invited. The dining-room was a bare, sombre room, where the Collector took his meals in solitary state and entertained half a dozen men to simple but well-cooked dinners, after which the table-cloth was removed from the polished dark mahogany, and the sound old port coasted round in silver slides. As the minister entered the dimly lit lobby everything seemed to him significant and eloquent: the middle-aged housekeeper with her air of severe propriety; the hat-stand, with no careless, unkempt exuberance of undress hats, shooting caps, country sticks, but with two silk hats only, one for good weather and Sundays, one for bad and funerals; a bamboo cane, with an ivory and silver head of straight and unadorned pattern; and two coats, one for cold, one for milder temperature. His sitting-room, where he spent his unofficial time, seemed to the minister that evening the very embodiment of the man—a physical shape, as it were, revealing his character. There was no comfortable disorder of papers, books, pipes, which sets one at ease in some rooms. Everything had its place; and the daily paper, after having been read, was sent down to the kitchen, unless there was some news of an unedifying description, in which case it was burned. Instead of a couch whereon one could lie and meditate after dinner on the problems of existence, there were two straight-backed arm-chairs, one on each side of the fireplace. The bookcase had glass doors, and one could read the titles on one shelf: *The Incidence of the Income Tax, The Abolition of the Malt Duty, Rules for the Collectors of H.M. Inland Revenue, Practice of the Free Church of Scotland, Abstract of the Acts of Assembly,* 1700 *to* 1840, and *The Elder's Manual.* The Collector was reading another book of the same genial and exhilarating class, and the minister noticed its contents with some dismay, *The Authority of Kirk Sessions;* but the Collector was quite cordial (for him).

"I am much pleased to see you, Mr. Rutherford, and should be gratified if your onerous duties allowed you to call more frequently; but I never forget that while our hours in the service of the

Queen are, as a rule, fixed, yours, in a higher service, have no limit. Do not, I pray you, sit there; that is in the draught between the door and the fire: here, if you will be so good, opposite me. Well, sir, how is your work prospering?"

The minister explained that he had intended to call sooner, but had been occupied with various cases of sickness, one of which had touched him closely. The people were not in the Collector's district; but perhaps he might have noticed them: they sat before him in church.

"Do you refer to a couple who have come quite recently, within a year, and who, as I judge, are newly married? They are interesting young people, it seemed to me, and most attentive, as I can testify, to their religious duties."

"Yes, the same. They were engaged for many years—a love affair of childhood, and they have been married less than eight months. They have a beautiful little home at Craigie, and they simply lived one for another."

"I can believe that, Mr. Rutherford; for I may mention that on one occasion, when you touched on love in appropriate and . . . somewhat moving terms, I happened to notice, without espionage I trust, that the wife slipped her hand into her husband's, and so they sat until the close of the sermon. Has trouble come to them?" and the Collector looked anxiously at the minister over his spectacles.

"Very dangerous and sudden trouble, I am sorry to say. Last Monday Mrs. Fortune was prematurely confined, and I . . . don't understand about these things; but the doctor considered it a very bad case."

"There had been complications, I fear; that sometimes happens, and, I don't know why, often with those whose lives are most precious. How is she? I earnestly hope that she . . . that he has not lost his bride." And Rutherford was struck by the anxiety and sadness in the Collector's voice.

"It was feared he might, and I have never seen any man so utterly broken down; and yet he kept calm for her sake. On Wednesday I stayed with him all the afternoon, and then I returned for the night after the prayer meeting."

"You were never more needed, be sure of that, sir; and is there hope of her recovery? I pray God, if it be His will, that the young wife be spared. Sitting before me has given me . . . an interest in the case." The Collector felt as if he must apologise for his unusual emotion.

"Their own doctor took a gloomy view, but they called in Dr. Manley. If there's real danger of death in Muirtown, or a radius of twenty miles, people must have Manley. And when he came into the parlour—you know his brusque, decided way —Manley turned to poor Fortune, who couldn't say one word, only look."

"It is, Mr. Rutherford, I will dare to say, the bitterest hour in all human sorrow"—the Collector spoke with strong feeling—" and Dr. Manley said?"

"'You thought you were going to lose your wife. No wonder; very bad case; but you're not, please God you're not. Dr. Gellatly knows his business. Mrs. Fortune will get better with care, mark me, immense care.' That's his way, you know, Collector; then Fortune . . . well, lost command of himself. So Manley went on,—'with care and skill; and Gellatly will see to that.'"

"God be praised!" exclaimed the Collector. "How many Dr. Manley has comforted in Muirtown! yet all medical skill is of no avail sometimes. But you have said nothing of the child."

"Manley was very doubtful about it—a girl, I think—and that is the only danger now with Mrs. Fortune. She is always asking for the child, which she has not seen; and so long as the news are good she is satisfied; but if the baby dies, it will go hard with the mother. Collector," cried Rutherford suddenly, "what mothers suffer, and how they love!"

The Collector took off his spectacles and examined them carefully, and then he wiped his eyes.

"When can the doctors be certain about the child, Mr. Rutherford?"

"Dr. Manley is going again this evening, and we hope he will be able to give a good report. I intended to call after seeing you; for if all be well, we would return thanks to God; and if . . . the child is not to live, there will be the more need of prayer. You will excuse me, Collector?"

"Go at once, sir, and . . . do you mind me going with you—just to the door, you know? I would sleep better to-night if I knew mother and child were safe." And the Collector was already moving to the door as one in haste.

"It is very good of you, Collector, and Fortune will value your sympathy; but there is something I called to talk about, and in my concern about Mrs. Fortune I . . . quite forgot it. It's about that unfortunate Sabbath-school entertainment."

"It's of no importance beside this trial—none whatever. Let us not delay, and I'll hear you on the other matter as we cross the South Meadow." So Rutherford was hustled out of the house in growing amazement.

"Let me say, first of all, Collector, that we are all much concerned . . ."

"Who could be otherwise, my good sir, if he had a heart in his bosom—only eight months married, and in danger of being separated. Mother and child taken, and the husband . . . left desolate . . . desolate for life!"

"If you could see your way," resumed Rutherford, after a respectful pause, and still harking back to the dispute, "to do anything . . ."

"Why did you not say that before? Only tell me; and if it be in my power, it shall be done. May I undertake the doctor's fees, or arrange with the nurse—through you of course, and in any way that will be in keeping with their feelings? Command me; I shall count it more than a privilege—a duty of pity and . . . love."

"It was not the Fortunes I was thinking of," said Rutherford; "but that can be left over. It is kind of you to offer help, they are not, however, in need of pecuniary assistance. Fortune has a good post in the railway. He's a first-rate engineer and a rising man. But if you cared to send flowers . . ."

"I am obliged to you for the hint, and I'll attend to this to-morrow morning." (The invalid had a fresh bouquet every day for a month.) "No, I will not go in. Just present my compliments and sympathy to Mr. Fortune. Here is my card, and . . . I'll just wait for the bulletin, if you would be so good as to come with it to the door."

"Baby's going to live too, and Manley says she will be a thumping big child in a few months!"

"Thank God, Mr. Rutherford! You cannot imagine how this incident has affected me. I'll go home now, and as I cross through the darkness of the Meadow my humble thanksgiving will mingle with yours, that in this home it has been God's pleasure to turn the darkness . . . into light." The voice of the Collector was charged with emotion, and Rutherford was confirmed in his romantic belief, although it seemed as if he had laboured in vain in the affair of the Sabbath school.

It was known before the meeting of that evening that no compromise had been effected; and when the Collector rose to speak, his face and manner charged with solemnity, it was felt that a crisis in the Free North had arrived. He began by saying that the subject of last meeting had never been long out of his thoughts, and that he had now arrived at a decision which commended itself to his judgment, and which he would submit with all brevity.

"Moderator"—for the Collector's historical utterance must be given in his own words—"if a man lives alone for many years, through the providence of God, and has come almost to the limit of ordinary human life as set down by the Psalmist, he is apt to become censorious and to be out of sympathy with young people; and if I have erred in this respect, you will kindly assign it to the habits of my life, not to the feelings of my heart."

There was so much gracious tenderness and unaffected humility in the Collector's tone that the grocer—unless roused, himself the most generous of men—wished to rise and withdraw the oranges instantly, and to leave the other details of tea and cantata absolutely to the Collector's decision, but was checked by the Moderator.

"So far, therefore, as I am concerned, I beg,

INCONSISTENCY 295

Moderator, to withdraw all opposition to the programme of my excellent friends, and I do so with all my heart; but, with your permission, I must annex one condition, which I hope my good friends will see their way to grant."

"Whatever the Collector wants shall be done!" burst in the Councillor, with chorus of applause from his side.

"Mr. Councillor must not be too rash lest he be caught in a snare," resumed the Collector facetiously, " for I am contemplating an innovation. However agreeable an evening entertainment in winter may be to the Vennel children, it appears to me that it would be even better for them to go to the country and admire the works of the Creator. There is a beautiful spot, only some twelve miles from here, which few Muirtown people have seen. I refer to the Tochty woods, where are the graves of Bessie Bell and Mary Gray, and my condition is that in the height of summer our poor Muirtown children be driven there and spend a long summer's day on the grass and by the river. I have only to add that if this proposal should meet with my friends' and my colleagues' approval, I shall count it a privilege and, er . . . honour to defray the cost." And for the first time in his public life the Collector sat down covered with confusion as with a garment.

The Tochty excursion came off on midsummer day, and is now a chapter of ancient history, to which what remains of the "old Guard" turn back with fond recollection; for though the things reported were almost incredible in Muirtown, yet were they all less than true. How there had been preparation in the unsavoury homes of the Vennel for weeks before, with the result that the children appeared in such spotless cleanliness and varied gaiety of attire that the Councillor was filled with pride, and the Collector declared that they looked like ladies and gentlemen. How the Collector was himself dressed in a light-grey summer suit, with a blue tie and a soft hat—this was never believed in his "Collection," but could any one have invented it?—and received many compliments on his appearance from all sides. How he had provided a barouche from the Kilspindie Arms for the Councillor and his wife, as chiefs of the school, and for his guests the Fortunes, whose baby crowed triumphantly half the way, and smiled in her sleep the other half; but the Collector travelled on the box-seat of the first break with the children—I tremble while I write—through the main streets of Muirtown. How the Collector had arranged with Burnbrae, the Free Kirk elder of Drumtochty, to supply every one on arrival with a pint of sweet, fresh milk; and how a quarrel arose in the end of the days between the town and country elders because Burnbrae gave the bairns a pint and a half at the price of a pint, and was never brought to a state of repentance. How almost every game known to children in ancient and modern times was played that day in Tochty woods, and the Collector patronised them all, from "tig" to "jingo-ring," with great access of popularity, if not conspicuous proficiency. How they all gathered together in front of the Lodge before leaving, and the Councillor—he has since risen to be Lord Provost—made the great speech of his life in proposing a vote of thanks to the Collector; and the Collector, to save himself from breaking down, called for three cheers in honour of the Councillor, and led them himself. And how they drove back past Kilbogie in the pleasant evening-time, and at the dispersing half the children of the Vennel shook hands with H.M. Collector of Inland Revenue for Muirtown.

The Collector returned home, his heart full of peace, and went to a certain closet of his bedroom, wherein was a box he had not opened for forty years. Within it lay a bridal dress, and an unfinished set of baby clothes, with a needle still fastened in the hem of a garment. And the Collector wept; but his tears were half sorrow and half joy, and he did not sorrow as one who had no hope.

FATHER JINKS

I

When I give him this title, I am perfectly aware that his right to it was at the best very doubtful, and that the Romans at St. Francis Xavier's laughed openly at his conceit; but he was always greatly encouraged by any one calling him "Father"; and now that he is gone I, for one, who knew both his little eccentricities and his hard sacrifices, will not throw stones at his grave—plenty were thrown at himself in his lifetime—nor shall I wound his memory by calling him Mr. Jinks. My opinion, as a layman, unattached and perhaps not even intelligent, is of very small account, but it is that of many other laymen; and to us it is of no importance what the servant of the Master is called, whether, like my dear old friend Father Pat Reilly, who has brought back more prodigals from the far country and rescued more waifs from the streets than any man I can hear of, or after the fashion of that worthy man, Pastor John Jump, as he delights to describe himself, who attends to business all the week—some-

FATHER JINKS

I

When I give him this title, I am perfectly aware that his right to it was at the best very doubtful, and that the Romans at St. Francis Xavier's laughed openly at his conceit; but he was always greatly encouraged by any one calling him "Father"; and now that he is gone I, for one, who knew both his little eccentricities and his hard sacrifices, will not throw stones at his grave—plenty were thrown at himself in his lifetime—nor shall I wound his memory by calling him Mr. Jinks. My opinion, as a layman, unattached and perhaps not even intelligent, is of very small account, but it is that of many other laymen; and to us it is of no importance what the servant of the Master is called, whether, like my dear old friend Father Pat Reilly, who has brought back more prodigals from the far country and rescued more waifs from the streets than any man I can hear of, or after the fashion of that worthy man, Pastor John Jump, as he delights to describe himself, who attends to business all the week—something in tinned meats, I think—and on Sunday preaches to a congregation of "baptized believers" with much force and earnestness, also without money or price. Both the Father and the Pastor had some doubts about my salvation—the one because I was not a member of the Anglican Communion, and the other because I was not a "strait Baptist"; but I never had any doubt about theirs —much less indeed than they had of one another's —and of the two I liked . . . but no, there is no use of comparisons, especially as the Pastor, as well as the Father, has gone to the land where, doubtless, many surprises are waiting for us all.

Nor does it seem of grave concern to some of us—but here again we may only be displaying our own ignorance of ecclesiastical subtleties— how a minister of religion is set apart to his office, if so be that he is an educated man and does the work put to his hand faithfully. Jinks was priested—I think that was what he called it, but he is not responsible for my mistakes—in a cathedral by a Right Rev. Father in God, and he used often to insist that only through such a channel could the grace of Orders come; but when the successor of the apostles advised Jinks in a most kindly, fatherly spirit to cease from some of his amiable extravagances—he had added a bran-new chasuble to his other bravery, which greatly pleased his female devotees—"the dear Father do look so pretty in his new chalice," one of his admirers said—Jinks repaid the Episcopal counsel with thinly-veiled scorn, and preached a sermon which ran to the unwonted length of twenty minutes to show that the bishop was himself a lawbreaker and little better than a Protestant.

My friend Carmichael, again, was ordained in the little Free Kirk of Drumtochty by the Presbytery of Muirtown,—that heavy body of Church Law and Divinity, Dr. Dowbiggin, being Moderator—and I cannot recollect Carmichael once referring to his Orders but he regarded his spiritual superiors with profound respect, and was very much relieved when his heresy case was dismissed —knowing very well that if they took it into their heads he would be turned out of his Church without delay and deposed from the ministry beyond human remedy. Carmichael was in the custom of denouncing priestcraft, and explaining that he had no claim to be a priest; but he administered a ghostly discipline so minute and elaborate, with sins which could be loosed by him, and reserved sins which could only be loosed by a higher authority, that the Father would have regarded it with envy. And Carmichael exercised an unquestioned authority among the hard-headed and strong-willed people of Drumtochty which Jinks would have cheerfully given ten years of his life to possess in the parish of St. Agatha's. Between the two there was this difference, that the vicar of St. Agatha's had the form of authority without the power, and the minister of Drumtochty had the power of authority without the form; and, as no man could be personally more humble or in heart more sincere than Jinks, this was the weary pity of the situation for my little Father.

Had St. Agatha's been in the West End, where his ritualism would have been accepted with graceful enthusiasm because it was fashionable—which would, however, have caused him much searching of heart: or in the East End, where it would have been condoned with a wink on account of his almsgiving, which would have wounded him deeply —Father Jinks had not been a subject of mockery and reproach. As it was Providence had dealt severely with the good man in sending him to the obdurate and stiff-necked parish of St. Agatha's, where the people were anything but open soil for his teaching. The houses ranged from twenty pounds of rent up to forty, and were inhabited by foremen artisans, clerks, shopkeepers, single women letting lodgings, and a few people retired on a modest competence. The district had not one rich man, although it was wonderful what some of the shopkeepers gave to special efforts at their chapels, nor any person in the remotest contact with society, but neither were there any evil livers or wastrels. Every one worked hard, lived frugally—with a special Sunday dinner —paid his taxes promptly, as well as his other debts, and lived on fairly good terms with his neighbours. The parish had certainly no enthusiasms, and would not have known what an ideal was, but it had a considerable stock of common sense, and most people possessed a traditional creed which they were prepared to defend with much obstinacy. St. Agatha's parish was a very home of Philistinism, and, as everybody knows, the Philistines have always had an instinctive dislike to Catholic usages and teachings.

II

The congregation of St. Agatha's were a prejudiced people, and had long been established in their own ways. The previous vicar, who had a certain fame as an orator of the florid order and rose to be an honorary canon, was a churchman of the lowest depths, and did things which Father Jinks used to mention with a shudder. He preached in a black gown, and delighted to address religious meetings in unlicensed places without any gown at all; he administered the Sacrament of the Lord's Supper once a month, and preferred to do so at evening service; he delighted to offer an extempore prayer before sermon, and never concluded a discourse without witnessing against the errors of the Church of Rome; he delighted in a three-decker pulpit, and would occasionally, in visiting the church for a baptism, leave his hat on the communion table where there was no other ornament. In his early days the music was led by a barrel organ, which was turned by the clerk, and later, when a large harmonium was introduced, the Psalms were read —the clerk leading the congregation with a stentorian voice—and Moody and Sankey's hymns were freely used. It was understood that the Canon had received a sudden call to the ministry while engaged in commercial pursuits, and had not found time for a University education—the hood which he wore at marriages was an invention of his wife's—and he was therefore very careful to correct the inaccuracies of the accepted versions, saying, with much impressiveness, "In the original Hebrew of this Gospel," or, "The Greek of Isaiah has it," although, in order to prevent monotony, he would next Sunday reverse the order of languages and again conform to traditional belief. Critical persons, connected by blood with the families of St. Agatha's and attending services there on occasion, declared openly that the Canon was a preposterous personage and a wind-bag; but he had without doubt a certain vein of genuine piety, which unsympathising people were apt to call unctuous, but which was, at any rate, warm; and a turn for rhetoric—he was of Irish birth—which might not be heavily charged with thought, but was very appetizing to the somewhat heavy minds of St. Agatha's parish. While he did not allow excessive charity to interfere with comfortable living, and while he did not consider it his duty to risk a valuable life by reckless visitation of persons with contagious diseases, the Canon, by his popular religious manner—his funeral addresses which he delivered at the grave, wearing a tall hat and swaying an umbrella, moved all to open grief,—and by his sermons,—an hour long and rich in anecdotes—held the parish in his hand and kept St. Agatha's full. People still speak of a course of lectures on "The Antichrist of the Bible," in which Rome was compared to Egypt, Samaria, Nineveh, Babylon, and the strangers sat in the aisles; and there can be no doubt that the Canon convinced the parish that a High Churchman was a Jesuit in disguise, and that a priest was (probably) an immoral person. So far as I could gather, the worthy man believed everything he said—although his way of saying it might savour of cant —and he was greatly impressed by an anonymous letter threatening his life and telling him that the eye of Rome was on him. He had been guided to marry three times—possibly as a protest against celibacy—with cumulative financial results of a fairly successful character, and his last wife mourns her loss at Cheltenham, where she subscribes freely to "escaped nuns," and greedily anticipates the field of Armageddon.

When the new patron, who had bought his position for missionary purposes, appointed the Rev. John James Jinks to be vicar of St. Agatha's, there was a rebellion in the parish, which, of course, came to nothing, and an appeal to the Bishop, which called forth a letter exhorting every person to peace and charity. Various charges were made against the new vicar, ranging from the fact that he had been curate in a church where the confessional was in full swing, and that the morals of the matrons of

St. Agatha's would be in danger, to the wicked calumny that he was an ex-Primitive Methodist, and was therefore, as is natural in such circumstances, very strong on the doctrine of apostolical succession. As the last insinuation cut Jinks to the quick, and was, indeed, almost the only attack he really felt, it is due to his memory to state that he was the son (and only child) of a country rector, whose living was worth £129, and who brought up his lad in the respectable, if somewhat arid, principles of the historical High Church school, which in the son blossomed rapidly into the luxuriance of Ritualism. It was only by the severest economy at the Rectory that Jinks could be sent to one of the cheaper Halls at Oxford, and it was the lasting sorrow of his blameless life that the Rector and his wife both died before he secured his modest pass degree. His mother used to call him John James, and had dreams that he would be raised to the Episcopate long after she had been laid to rest; but he knew very well from the beginning that his intellectual gifts were limited, and that his career would not be distinguished. While he magnified his priestly office beyond bounds, and was as bold as a lion for the Church in all her rights and privileges, he had no ambition for himself and was the most modest of men. Because he was only five feet four in height, and measured thirty-two inches round the chest, and had a pink and white boyish face, and divided his hair down the middle, and blushed when he was spoken to by women and dons, and stammered slightly in any excitement, they called him Jinksy at Tommy's Hall, and he answered cheerfully; and when our big Scots doctor availed himself on occasion of the same familiar form of address he showed no resentment. No one, however, could say, when he was with us in St. Agatha's, that he forgot his position, not only as a priest with power to bind and loose, but also as the disciple of his Lord; for if any clergyman ever did, our little Father adorned the doctrine of Christ by his meekness and lowliness of character, and by a self-sacrifice and self-forgetfulness which knew no limits. He wore a low-crowned, broad-brimmed hat, and in winter a garment resembling a Highland cloak, which gave him as he imagined a certain resemblance to a continental abbé; and as he skimmed at all hours along our sombre, monotonous streets on errands which were often very poorly requited, and in many cases may have been quite uncalled for, he was, if you pleased to see him from a certain angle, a rather absurd figure; but as his simple, boyish face grew thinner and paler every month, and his eyes grew brighter and more spiritual, one's smile rather passed into the tears of the heart. And now that he is gone, and no one in St. Agatha's is vexed either by his chasuble or his kindness, it comes to us that Father Jinks followed the light given to him without flinching, and has rendered in a good account.

III

When Father Jinks read himself into St. Agatha's, the church seemed to him little better than a conventicle, a mere preaching-house, and it was his business to change it into a place fit for Catholic worship. His success in this direction was marvellous. Before his death there was a chancel with screen and choir stalls, a side pulpit of carved stone with scenes from the Gospels thereon, a reredos, and an altar with cross and candlesticks, besides other pieces of ecclesiastical furniture of lesser importance and beyond the lay intelligence. There was also an organ, for which so many pews were removed, and a font near the door, for which other pews were removed, and an east window, containing the life and death of our patron saint, about whom nobody knew anything before, and for which a magnificent geometrical design in red and blue, greatly admired by the parish, had to be removed. The very plaster, with ornate pattern of roses, he had stripped from the roof, and had the oak laid bare; and although the walls had been tastefully decorated by a local firm with a mixed border on a ground of green, so fierce and unrelenting was the Vicar's iconoclastic passion that this also was sacrificed, and nothing was to be seen in St. Agatha's save stone and wood. "It was the 'omeliest church you ever see," that excellent woman Mrs. Judkin remarked to me, "in the old Canon's time, with the bits of colour, and 'im looking down at you in 'is black gown; and now it chills your 'art to sit there let alone that you're hexpected to bow 'alf the time," and so Mrs. Judkin, with many of like mind, went off to Ebenezer, where the firmament was represented on the roof and the service was decidedly warm. The structural reformation (or deformation, as it was generally considered) was a very achievement of persevering and ingenious begging, in which he taxed the patron and all the patron's friends, as well as every old lady or ecclesiastical layman with the reputation of highness, obtaining a pulpit from one and a font from another, picking up crosses, candlesticks, stools, altar-cloths in all quarters, and being mightily cheered by every addition to the full equipment of this neglected edifice. Nor did Father Jinks ask from other people what he would not give himself, for he dispensed with a curate that he might repair the chancel, and, as appeared afterwards, he expended all his little patrimony on the apocryphal life of St. Agatha, whose doings and appearance as represented on that window were a subject of derision to the wits of the parish. When Jinks held his first festival in her honour, and preached a discourse eleven minutes in length on St. Agatha's example and miracles, an interesting correspondence followed in the local paper, in which it was asserted that the church, then in the country and a chapel of ease to the famous church of St. Paul's-in-the-Fields, was named in the evil Laudian times, and ought to have been rechristened by the name of Wycliffe or Latimer in the days of the late lamented Canon; that St. Agatha never existed; that if she did, she was a Papist; that if we knew enough, we should likely find that her antecedents were very doubtful.

This correspondence, in which my friend himself was freely handled, did not in the least disturb him, for the Festival of St. Agatha was a height to which he had been working for the three years, and it was the last function of his public ministry. When the procession came out of the vestry, with a cross-bearer—Jack Storgiss, the grocer, to whose deformed little boy Jinks had been very kind—the banners of the Guild of St. Agatha, a choir of six men and twelve boys in varied garments, Father Jinks himself with everything on he knew, attended by acolytes—two little monkeys on whose ingenuous countenances self-importance struggled with mischief—and, having marched round the church singing "Onward, Christian soldiers," reentered the chancel, so far as outward things went, the Father's heart was almost satisfied; and as, in his stall, he thought of the desolation of the past he was as one that dreamed.

If Jinks allowed himself to be proud of anything, it was of his choir; and when people spoke of my friend as a weakling because he was insignificant in appearance and a feeble preacher—he himself thanked God daily that he was a priest, to whom Pastor Jumps' oratorical gifts were unnecessary—one could always point to the choir, for the qualities which created and held together that remarkable body were peculiar to Jinks and were quite wanting in the Pastor. Three years before this advertisement had appeared in the *Anglo-Catholic*:—

"Wanted, an organist and choirmaster, who will be prepared, for the glory of God and the love of sacred music, to assist a priest in affording Catholic worship to a neglected parish."

This unworldly invitation caught the eye (and fancy) of Harold de Petre—his original name was Henry Peter—about whom his friends were much concerned because he had a small competency and would do nothing except work at music; because he wore a brown velvet coat and a loose red bow, and three ancient gems on his left hand, and his hair falling over his ears; and because he practised a certain luxurious softness of life which might pass any day into positive vice. Two more different men could not have been found in a day's journey, but they became friends at once. The priestly instinct detected at once in Petre a gift whose concentration would be the salvation of a soul and an assistance to the Church of God; and the humility and sincerity of the little priest were very attractive to the æsthete. From that time the curiously assorted pair worked together in perfect harmony and ever-growing affection, with one common desire to beautify the worship and edifice of St. Agatha's. In order to secure an organ Petre sacrificed one-third of his means, and was daily designing some improvement in his loved instrument; for her help he had even learned some organ handicraft, and could be seen almost any day toiling in his shirt sleeves. As he watched the life of the Vicar, Petre began also to make many personal sacrifices, giving up his wine—used to spend a good deal on Chateau Lafitte—to defray choir expenses; teaching the piano in the more ambitious homes of the parish, and with the proceeds providing two tenors and two basses of distinction for the choir. One year he took no holiday that the altar might be becomingly dressed according to the season of the Church year, whether of joy or sorrow. Working with Jinks, a certain change even came over Petre's outer man; with every year he shed a gem; black velvet replaced the brown, and his hair became almost decorous; and one evening, when the two were having a lemon squash after hard work at the Easter decorations, Petre made a confession to his friend.

"There is something I wanted to tell you, Jinks," lighting his pipe slowly, "My name is not really

Harold de Petre: it's . . . just Henry Peter. Didn't sound very artistic, you know, and I just . . . improved it in fact. Rather think that I should go back to old signature."

"My own name," said the Vicar with much simplicity, "isn't a high-class name, and I was once tempted to change it—it lends itself too easily to abbreviations—but it seemed unreal to do that kind of thing."

"Do you know, Father, I expect that anthem to go well to-morrow; that little rascal Bags took the high notes magnificently to-night. I told him so, and he was awfully pleased: he's as keen as mustard at practice."

Nothing further was said about fancy pseudonyms, but next time the Father saw the organist's signature it was Henry Peter.

The boys in St. Agatha's choir were not angels, but they were Jinks' particular friends, and would do more for him than for their own parents. He had picked them up one by one in the parish as he visited—for he had no school—upon the two qualifications that each one had an ear, and each was an out-and-out boy. Because he was so good himself Jinks would have nothing to do with prigs and smugs; and because he did nothing wrong himself he delighted in the scrapes of his boys. It was to him they went in trouble, and he somehow found a way of escape. Every one knew who paid for the broken glass in the snowball fight between Thackeray and Dickens Streets, in which Bags and another chorister, much admired for his angelic appearance, led their neighbourhood; and it was asserted by the Protestant party that the Papist Vicar was seen watching the fray from the corner. When an assistant School Board master bullied his boys beyond endurance and they brought him to his senses with pain of body, it was the Vicar of St. Agatha's who pled the case of the rebels before the Board, and saved them from public disgrace and the Police Court. The Vicarage and all its premises were at the disposal of the boys, and they availed themselves freely of their privileges. Bags kept his rabbits in the yard—his parents allowed no such tenants at home—and his fellow-warrior of the snowball fight had a promising family of white mice in one of the empty rooms, where another chorister had a squirrel, and *his* friend housed four dormice. There was a fairly complete collection of pigeons —tumblers, pouters, fantails; you could usually have your choice in pigeons at the Vicarage of St. Agatha's. The choir did elementary gymnastics in what was the Canoness's drawing-room, and learned their lessons, if they were moved that way, in the dining-room. Every Friday evening, after practice, there was a toothsome supper of sausages and mashed potatoes, with stone ginger. Ye gods, could any boy or man feed higher than that? On Saturdays in summer the Vicar took the whole gang to the nearest park, where, with some invited friends, they made two elevens and played matches, with Jinks, who was too short-sighted to play himself, but was the keenest of sportsmen, as consulting umpire; and on chief holidays they all made excursions into the country, when Harold de Petre became Henry Peter with a vengeance. And this was how there was no difficulty in getting boys for the choir, and people began to come to hear the music at St. Agatha's.

IV

It is not to be supposed that Father Jinks achieved his heart's desire without opposition, and he verified in his experience the fact that a man's bitterest foes are those of his own household. He was opposed by the people's churchwarden, who would not go elsewhere, declaring that he had been in St. Agatha's before Jinks was born—which was not the case—and would be after Jinks had gone, which turned out sadly true. He was harassed by "aggrieved parishioners," who declared by petitions in all quarters that they could no longer worship in St. Agatha's, and that what with daily services, fine music, and decorations, the place was little better than a Papist chapel. His breakfast-table had daily one or two anonymous letters reminding Jinks of his ordination vows, and accusing him of perjury, insinuating charges against his moral character and threatening exposure, quoting texts regarding the condition of the unconverted and the doom of hypocrites. He was dragged before all kinds of Courts, this one little man, and received every form of censure and admonition; he was ordered to prison, and left the Vicarage one evening in a cab, while the choir boys, led by Bags, wanted to fight the officer. And when all these measures produced no effect, more forcible measures were taken to express the mind of the people and to re-establish the Reformation in the parish of St. Agatha's. A leader was raised up in a gentleman who had earned an uncertain living by canvassing for the *Kings of England* in forty-two parts, in selling a new invention in gas-burners, in replying to infidels in Hyde Park, and in describing the end of the world with the aid of a magic lantern. This man of varied talents saw it to be his duty—and who can judge another man's conscience?—to attend St. Agatha's one Sunday forenoon, accompanied by a number of fellow-Protestants, who, owing to the restriction of the licensing laws, were out of employment at that hour, and they expressed their theological views during service in a very frank and animated fashion. Bigger men than Jinks might have been upset by the turmoil and menaces; but it shows what a spirit may dwell in small bulk, that this shy modest man did not stutter once that morning, and seemed indeed unconscious of the "Modern Luther's" presence; and after the floor of the church had been washed on Monday no trace remained that a testimony had been lifted up against the disguised Jesuit who was corrupting St. Agatha's. Once only did Jinks publicly reply to the hurricane of charges which beat upon him during his short, hard service, and that was when he was accused of having introduced the confessional, with results which it was alleged were already well known in the district, and which would soon reduce its morality to the social level of the south of Ireland. A week afterwards Jinks explained in a sermon which he had rewritten three times: (1) That the practice of confession was, in his poor judgment, most helpful to the spiritual life by reminding us of the sins which do most easily beset us, and their horrible guilt before God; (2) That it was really the intention of the Church of England that her children should have this benefit; and (3) That he, John James Jinks, a duly ordained priest of the same Church, had power, under conditions, to hear confessions and declare the forgiveness of sins to all true penitents. Thereafter, he went on to state that he had not introduced confession as a practice in St. Agatha's, because he had never been trained in confessional theology, because a confessor required authority from his bishop, and this the bishop would not give; and, finally, it seemed to him that any confessor must be a priest with a special knowledge of life, and of conspicuous holiness; and, as they knew well, he was neither, but only an ignorant and frail man, who was more conscious of his deficiencies every day, and who earnestly besought the aid of their prayers. This sermon was reported in the *Islington Mercury*, which circulated largely amongst us, and called forth an ingenious reply from the "Modern Luther," who pointed out that if Mr. Jinks had not set up a confessional box in St. Agatha's church, it was only because his (the "Modern Luther's") eye was upon him; that the confessional could likely be discovered in the Vicarage; that in so far as Mr. Jinks was not telling the truth he would receive absolution from the Jesuits, and that he very likely had already received a license to tell as many lies as he saw would help his cause. Men, however, do count for something even in religious controversy, and the very people who had no belief in Jinks' doctrine could see some difference between his patient, charitable, self-sacrificing life and the career of a windbag like the "Modern Luther," and no one in the last year of his life accused Jinks of falsehood.

During all these troubled days he never lost his temper, or said bitter things: he believed, as he once told me in all modesty, that if he suffered it was for his sins, and that persecution was only a call to harder labour; and it appeared afterwards that he had gone out of his way to do a good turn to certain of his bitterest enemies. Indeed, I am now certain that they did not injure him at all; but one is also quite as certain that he was hindered and made ridiculous by certain of his own supporters. Certain young women of uncertain age who had been district visitors and carried tracts under the revered Canon, or had been brought up in various forms of Dissent, responded with enthusiasm to the Catholic Reformation. They wore large gold (or gilt) crosses, and were careful to use heavily crossed prayer-books; they attended early celebration, and were horrified at people taking the sacrament not fasting; they not only did obeisance to the altar, where there was no sacrament, and bowed at the name of Jesus, and crossed themselves in a very diligent and comprehensive fashion, but invented forms of devotion which even Jinks could not comprehend, and so scandalized the old clerk, who stuck by St. Agatha's, that he asked them one day during service if they were ill, and suggested that they should leave the church before things came to the worst. Personally, as a close observer of this drama, I had no sympathy with the ill-natured suggestion that these devout females were moved by the fact that the priest of St. Agatha's was unmarried, because no man was ever more careful in his intercourse with the other sex than my friend, and because this kind of woman—till she marries, and with modifications afterwards—has a mania for ritual and priests. This band, who called themselves the Sisters of St. Agatha, and severely tried our unsentimental district, were a constant embarrassment to Jinks. They made the entire attendance at the daily services; they insisted on cleaning the chancel on their knees; they fluttered round the confused little man in the street; they could hardly be kept out of the Vicarage; they talked of nothing but saints' days and offices and vestments, till Jinks, the simplest and honestest of men, was tempted, for his sake and their own salvation, to entreat them to depart and return whence they had come.

V

The strongest and most honourable opponent the Vicar had was my other friend, Pastor Jump, who would not condescend to the methods or company of the "Modern Luther," but who was against both Jinks and Jinks' Church, whether it was Low, High, Broad, or anything else, on grounds of reason and conscience. He did not believe in creeds, whether they were made in Rome or Geneva, and considered a Presbyter just a shade better than a priest. His one book of theology was the Bible, which he knew from Genesis to Revelation in the English Version (he also knew far more about the Hebrew and Greek than the Canon did), and he found his ecclesiastical model in the Acts of the Apostles. It was indeed the Pastor's firm conviction that the Christian Church had only had two periods of purity in her history, one under the charge of the Apostle Paul, and the other under the Puritans; and that if, during her whole history, bishops and such like people had been replaced by Puritan ministers, it would have been much better for Christianity and for the world. His idea of a Christian was a person who knew the day that he had been converted, and who afterwards had been baptized; and of the Church, that it was so many of these people with a pastor to teach them. He detested Established Churches, priests, and liturgies, as well as the House of Lords, capitalists, and all privileged persons. His radicalism was however tempered by a profound belief in himself and his own opinions. He was fond of insisting on the rights of the masses; but when the working people wished to have the Park open on Sunday that they might walk there with their children, the Pastor fought them tooth and nail, and he regarded their desire to see pictures on Sunday as the inspiration of Satan. No man was ever more eloquent upon the principles of religious liberty, but he would have put an infidel into prison without compunction, and he drave forth a deacon from his own congregation with contumely, who held unsound views on the Atonement. The tyranny of the Papacy was a favourite theme at Ebenezer, as well as the insolence of priests; but every one knew that Pastor Jump as Pope was infallible without the aid of any Council, and that his little finger was heavier in personal rule than both Jinks' arms. When the Pastor, who had the voice of a costermonger and the fist of a prize-fighter, was carried away at a Liberation Society meeting by his own undoubted eloquence, and described himself as a conscientious Dissenter, despised by the proud priests of the Anglican Church, and next day one saw Jinks, thinner than ever, hurrying along the street, and concealing beneath his shabby cloak some dainty for a sick child, then one had a quite convincing illustration of the power and utility of rhetoric.

Upon occasion the Pastor felt it his duty to depart from his usual course of evangelical doctrine, and to enlighten his people on some historical subject, and the district was once shaken by a discourse on Oliver Cromwell, whom he compared to Elijah, and whose hatred of the Baal worship was held up for imitation in our own day. Jinks committed the one big mistake of his ministry by replying with a sermon on St. Charles the Blessed Martyr —I think he said St.—which was a very weak performance, and left the laurels altogether with Ebenezer. It must indeed be admitted that Jump exactly expressed the mind of an Englishman of the lower middle class, who understands the Evangelical system and no other, and likes extempore prayer, with its freedom, variety, warmth, and surprises, who suspects priests of wishing to meddle with his family affairs, and dislikes all official pretensions, although willing to be absolutely ruled by a strong man's personality. Both were extreme men, and both were needed to express the religious sense of an English parish. Jump considered the Canon an indefensible humbug, neither one thing nor another, and the Canon used to pass Jump on the street; but the Sunday after Jinks' death the Pastor, who had a warm heart in his big body, and testified of things he had seen, passed a eulogium on the late Vicar of St. Agatha's, so generous and affecting, that beside it the peeping little sermon preached in St. Agatha's by a " Father " of the " Anglican Friars " was as water to wine. The Pastor declared that although he did not agree with his doctrine, he knew no man who had lived nearer his Lord, or had done more good works than the Vicar of St. Agatha's; and that if every priest had been like him, he would never say a word against the class. The people heard his voice break as he spoke and two deacons wiped their eyes, and the angels set down the sermon in that Book where the record of our controversies is blotted out by their tears, and our deeds of charity are written in gold.

Perhaps, however, our poor priest suffered most in some ways at the hands of a handful of Scots who had settled in the parish. They did not oppose any of his proceedings, for they never condescended to cross the door of St. Agatha's, and they accepted any extravagances of ritual as things to be expected of an Episcopalian. Nor had they, like the Pastor, a hereditary feud with the Anglican Church, for neither they nor their fathers ever had anything to do with it. They were indeed inclined to believe that the Prayer-Book, where the officiating clergyman is called a Minister and a Priest alternately, is admirably suited to the English mind, to which the Almighty has been pleased to deny the gift of logic. What touched, and (almost) nettled, the little Father was the tacit and immovable superiority of the Scots, which made conversion impossible, and even pastoral conversation difficult. It was Jinks' conscientious conviction that he was responsible for the spiritual charge of all the people in the parish, and so he visited laboriously among the Scots schismatics, if haply he might bring them to the true faith, with mortifying results. Old Andrew MacKittrick seemed to Jinks' innocent mind a promising case, because Andrew had retired on a pension after keeping the books of a drysalter's firm for forty years, and now had nothing to do but argue. In fact, on the Vicar's first visit, the bookkeeper fairly smacked his lips, seeing whole afternoons of intellectual diversion before him; and Jinks, who was ever optimistic, already imagined the responsible-looking figure of the Scot sustaining a procession. It turned out a lamentable instance of cross-purposes, for Jinks was burning to prove, with all tenderness, that the Kirk had no Orders; while the idea that Dr. Chalmers was not a real minister and Archbishop Sharpe was, seemed to Andrew unworthy of discussion by any sane person; and Andrew, on his part, was simply longing for some one to attack Jonathan Edwards' *Freedom of the Will*, while Jinks had never heard of the book, and was quite blameless of philosophy. After two conferences, Andrew was sadly convinced of their futility, and would not waste time on a third,

"Jess wumman," he said to his housekeeper, rolling himself hurriedly up in a plaid and lying down on the sofa, "there's that curate body at the door again; a've nae satisfaction arguin' wi' him, for he's no fit to tak' up ony serious subject. Just say that a'm no feelin' verra weel the day, and, see here, slip ten shillings into his hand to gie awa', for he's a fine bit craturie amang the poor, but he's no head for argument."

With Mrs. Gillespie, who kept lodgings, and was as a mother to two Scots bank clerks pushing their way up to be managers, Father Jinks was not more successful, but his discomfiture was of another kind.

"Come in, come in; it's an awfu' day to be oot, an' ye dinna look strong; na, na, a dinna gang to Saint Agatha's, for ye ken we've a Kirk o' oor ain, an' a properly ordained minister, but a'm gled to see ye; a'm thankfu' for my ain preevileges, but a'm no bigoted.

"Sit doon there by the fire an' dry yersel; a cudna manage wi' a prayer-book masel, but we've had mony advantages in Scotland, and it suits the English fouk. A hed a cousin 'at married an Episcopalian, and she gied wi' him as long as he lived, though of course it was a deprivation.

"'A schismatic?'—a've heard the word: they used to misca' the English bishops that way in the North—an' ye called to warn me. Noo that was kind, and, of coorse, ye did na know that a sit under

Mr. McCaw; but Losh keep us! ye're juist dreeping; a'll get ye a pair o' the lad's slippers an' mak ye a warm cup o' tea.

"A hed a laddie juist your age, an' ma heart warms to young men that are na verra strong. Say awa'; a'll hear ye though a'm in the next room. There noo, drink up your tea, an' that's short-bread frae Edinburgh. Let's hear noo aboot yer Kirk; somebody was sayin' that ye carried on the same antics as the Papists; but a'm no believin' that. Are ye feelin' warmer noo, ma puir wee mannie?" and the good woman encompassed Jinks with motherly attentions, but refused to take seriously his efforts to convert her from the Kirk to the Church. Nor did he think it an encouraging sign that Mrs. Gillespie pressed him to give her "a cry" every time he was in the street, and sent him three pots of black currant jam for his chest.

The most disappointing encounter was with our Scots doctor, who had looked into St. Agatha's one evening in passing and found Jinks warning Dissenters of all kinds, among whom the Doctor found to his amusement that he was included of their doom if they died in schism. The Doctor's delight reached its height when Jinks, standing at his full height of five feet four, and looking more than ever like a dear little boy, opened his arms and invited every wandering prodigal to return to the bosom of Mother Church.

"Jinksy"—and the Doctor laid hold of the

Father next day on the street—"what sort of nonsense was yon ye were talking in your kirk last night?

"Hurt my feelings"—as Jinks was explaining that he had only been declaring the truth, and that he did not wish to offend any one—"it would take three men of your size to offend me. But I say, Jinksy, do you ever take a holiday in Scotland? You hope to do some day. Then I'll give ye a bit of advice: if you ever feel a turr-murring in your inside, take the first train for Carlisle. Why? Because if you die in Scotland, you'll die a Dissenter; and then, my little man, you know where you'll go to"; for the Doctor's hand in humour was heavy, and his style was that of an elephant crashing through a wood.

VI

Next time the Anglican and the Scot met it was in circumstances where differences of creed are forgotten and good men stand shoulder to shoulder. In one room of the house a clerk's wife was seriously ill with influenza, and in another the Doctor was examining her husband—a patient, hard working, poorly paid drudge, who had come home from the City very ill. "My wife thinks that it's nothing but a bad 'eadache. Don't tell 'er, Doctor, else it might go bad with 'er, an' she 'asn't much strength; but I say, tell me, 'aven't I got diphtheria?"

"What makes everybody that gets a sore throat think he has diphtheria? Well, I believe you have some grit in you, and don't want to be treated like a child. You have, I'm sorry to say, and pretty bad; but you have the spirit to make a fight, and I'll do my best.

"Yes, I'll see that no one in this house comes near you, and I'll try to get a nurse for to-night, but they're hard to get just now. I'll come back with medicine in half an hour; and, look here, Holmes, mind your wife and bairns, and keep up your heart.

"No, Jinks, you must not come into this house: it's more than influenza. Holmes has got diphtheria very bad; ought to have been in bed two days ago, but the stupid ass stuck to his work. The mischief is that I can't get a nurse, and he should not be left alone at night.

"You, man alive, you're no fit for such work, and you would maybe catch it . . . I know you're not afraid, but . . . well, its real gude o' ye, an' I'll see ye settled for the night about eight.

"That's the medicine, every three hours"—the doctor was giving his directions to Nurse Jinks in the sick-room—"and let him have some brandy and water when he's thirsty. Toots, Holmes, I know you could get a bottle for yourself, but this is a special brand for sick folk. Oh, yes, it'll go in the bill, risk me for that: every Scot looks after himself. The minister is to stay all night with you, and what between the two of us we'll see ye through.

"Here's a cordial for yourself, Jinks"—this outside the door—"and for ony sake keep clear of his breath. If he takes a turn for the worse, send the servant lass for me. I may be out, but they will know where to get me. And, Jinks, old man, I withdraw that about Carlisle. . . . Ye'll go to Heaven from either side o' the Tweed. God bless you, old man; you're doin' a good turn the night . . .

"Yes, he's much worse than he was last morning;

FATHER JINKS

but it's not the blame of your nursing: there's just one chance, and I'll try it. How do you know about it? Well, yes, if you must know, I am going to use suction. Get diphtheria myself? Maybe I may, and why should I not run the risk as well as you, Mr. Jinks? . . . It's all right, man. I'm not angry. Neither you nor me are cowards," said the Doctor; "neither is Holmes, and he must have his chance, poor chap. Yes, I would be glad of your help.

"No, you will not be needed at Holmes's to-night, and you've had enough of it, Jinks. I've got a nurse, and Holmes is coming round first rate. It's all right about paying the nurse; I'll see to that. Man, ye would pay for all the nurses in the district, if ye were allowed.

"Me, I'm as fit as a fiddle. Doctors can't afford to be ill; but you're no the thing, Jinks. Come back to the manse with me this minute, I want to have a look at ye. Yon were three hard nichts ye had"—the Doctor dropped into Scots when he was excited. . . .

"Sir Andrew's gone, and I wish we had better news for you and ourselves. Don't thank me for telling the truth; no man would tell you a lie. . . . You're all right, whatever happens, Jinks," and he dropped his hand within reach of the Father's, on whose face the shadow was fast falling.

"It will not be for some hours, may be not till morning, and I hope you'll not suffer much . . .

I'll come back after the minister has left and stay with you till, till . . ."

"Daybreak," said Jinks.

"Doctor," Jinks whispered, during the night as they watched by his bed, the Scot on one side and Peter, who would allow no nurse, on the other, "the Scots kirk has seemed to me . . . as Samaria, but the Lord chose . . . a Samaritan in his parable, and you are . . . that Samaritan," and the Father looked at the Doctor with eyes full of love. Just before sunrise he glanced at the Doctor enquiringly.

"Yes, it's no far off now, an' the worst's past. Ye'll have an easy passage." They passed each an arm round his neck, and each took one of his hands.

"Till Jesus comes Himself," whispered Jinks, thanking them with his eyes.

"O Saviour of the world, who by Thy cross and precious blood hast redeemed us, save us, and help us, we humbly beseech Thee, O Lord." This which he had often offered for others, he now prayed for himself very slowly. The light stole into the room and woke him from a brief unconsciousness.

"I believe" . . . he said, "in the Life Everlasting," and the soul of the faithful servant was with the Lord, Whom, not having seen, he had loved.

When the Doctor left the Vicarage, although still very early, Bags, the choir-boy, was on the doorstep and was weeping bitterly.

THE PASSING OF DOMSIE

THE PASSING OF DOMSIE

It was an ancient custom that Domsie and Drumsheugh should dine with Doctor Davidson in the Manse after the distribution of prizes at the school, and his companions both agreed afterwards that the Dominie was never more cheerful than on those days. There was always a review of stories when the Doctor and Domsie brought out their favourites, with Drumsheugh for an impartial and appreciative audience, and every little addition or improvement was noted in a spirit of appreciative criticism.

During the active operations of dinner, talk was disjointed and educational, hinging on the prospects of the calf crop in the school, and the golden glories of the past, ever better than the present, when the end of each University session showered medals on Drumtochty. When the Doctor had smacked his first glass of port, having examined it against the light, and the others had prepared their toddy in a careful silence, broken only by wise suggestions from the host, it was understood that genuine conversation might begin.

"Aye, aye," Domsie would remark, by way of intimating that they, being now in an open and genial mind, were ready to welcome one of the Doctor's best stories, and Drumsheugh became insistent.

"A'm no wantin' tae tribble ye, Docter, but ave never got ower that sermon on the turtle, Docter. Ye micht let's hear it again. A'm no sure gin the Dominie ever herd it." May Drumsheugh be forgiven!

Whereupon Domsie went on the back trail, and affected to search his memory for the traces of the turtle, with no satisfaction. May he also be forgiven!

"Toots, Drumsheugh, you are trying to draw my leg. I know you well, eh? As for you, Dominie, you've heard the story twenty times. Well, well, just to please you; but mind you, this is the last time.

"It was the beginning of a sermon that old MacFee, of Glenogil, used to preach on the Monday after the Sacrament from the text, 'The voice of the turtle is heard in the land,' and this was the introduction.

"There will be many wonders in the latter day; but this is the greatest of them all—the voice of the turtle shall be heard in the land. This marvel falls into two parts, which we shall consider briefly and in order.

"I. A new posture evidently implied, when an animal that has gone upon its belly for ages shall arise on its hind legs and walk majestically through the land, and

THE PASSING OF DOMSIE

"II. A new voice distinctly promised, when a creature that has kept silence from generation to generation will at last open its mouth and sing melodiously among the people."

"It's michty," summed up Drumsheugh, after the exposition had been fully relished. "Ye'll no hear the like o' that noo-a-days in a coonty. It's weel telt also, and that's important, for the best story is no worth hearin' frae a puir hand. The corn needs to be cleaned afore ye tak it tae market.

"The story is not without merit," and the Doctor's modesty was all the more striking as he was supposed to have brought the turtle into its present form out of the slenderest materials, "but the Dominie has some far neater things." Anything Domsie had was from Aberdeen, and not to be compared, he explained, with Perthshire work, being very dry and wanting the fruity flavour of the Midland County; but he could still recall the divisions of the action sermon given every year before the winter Sacrament in Bourtrie-Lister:

I. "Let us remember that there is a moral law in the universe."

II. "Let us be thankful there is a way of escape from it."

And then Domsie would chuckle with a keen sense of irony at the theology underneath. "For the summer Sacrament," he would add after a pause, "we had a discourse on sin wi' twa heads,

'Original Sin' and 'Actual Transgressions'; and after Maister Deuchar finished wi' the first, he aye snuffed, and said with great cheerfulness: 'Now let us proceed to actual transgressions.'"

Although Domsie's tales had never in them the body of the Doctor's, yet he told them with such a pawkie humour, that Drumsheugh was fain between the two to cry for mercy, being often reduced to the humiliation of open laughter, of which he was afterwards much ashamed.

On that day, however, when Domsie made his lamentable announcement, it was evident to his friends that he was cast down, and ill at ease. He only glanced at a Horace which the Doctor had been fool enough to buy in Edinburgh, and had treasured up for Domsie's delectation at the close of the school year—the kind of book he loved to handle, linger over, return to gaze at, for all the world like a Catholic with a relic.

"Printed, do you see, by Henry Stephen, of Paris; there's his trademark, a philosopher gathering twigs from the tree of knowledge—and bound by Boyet—old French morocco. There is a coat of arms—I take it of a peer of France;" and the Doctor, a born book-collector, showed all its points, as Drumsheugh would have expatiated on a three-year-old bullock.

Domsie could not quite resist the contagious enthusiasm; putting on his spectacles to test the printing; running his hand over the gold tooling

THE PASSING OF DOMSIE

as one strokes a horse's glossy skin, and tasting afresh one or two favourite verses from a Horace printed and bound by the master craftsmen of their day. But it was only a brief rally, and Domsie sank again into silence, from which neither kindly jest nor shrewd country talk could draw him, till at last the Doctor asked him a straight question, which was going far for us, who thought it the worst of manners to pry into one's secrets:

"What ails you, Dominie? Are any of your laddies going back on you?" and the Doctor covered the inquiry by reminding Drumsheugh that his glass was low.

"Na, na; they are fechting hard wi' body and mind, an' daein' their verra best, accordin' tae their pairts. Some o' the Drumtochty scholars lived and some dee'd in the war at the University, but there wasna ane disgraced his pairish."

"They have made it known in every University of Scotland," broke in the Doctor, "and also their master's name."

"Ye've aye made ower mickle o' my wark, but a'm grateful this nicht an' content to tak' a' ye say in yir goodness, for a've sent oot ma last scholar," and Domsie's voice broke.

"Not a bit of it. Man alive, you're fit for ten years yet, and as for laddies, I know four in the school that'll do you credit, or I'm not minister of Drumtochty."

"If it's the siller for their fees," began Drumsheugh, inwardly overcome by Domsie's unexpected breakdown.

Domsie waved his hand. "The laddies are there, and the twa or three notes 'ill be gotten as afore, but it 'ill no be me that 'ill feenish them."

"What is the meaning of this, Mister Jamieson?" demanded the Doctor sternly, for the woeful dejection of Domsie was telling on him also.

"It's been on ma mind for years to retire, an' maybe I should hae dune it lang syne; but it was hard on flesh an' blude. I hev taught ma last class, and ye will need to get another Dominie," and Domsie, who was determined to play the man, made a show of filling his glass, with a shaking hand.

"Ye're an Aiberdeenshire man a ken, though maist fouk hae forgotten that ye're no ain' o' oorsels, but div ye tell me that ye're gain' tae leave us after a' thae years an' a' the bairns ye've educat?" and Drumsheugh grew indignant.

"Dinna be feared, Drumsheugh, or think me ungrateful. I may gang north tae see ma birthplace aince mair, an' the graves o' ma fouk, an' there's another hoose in Aberdeen I would like tae see, and then I'm comin' back to Drumtochty to live an' dee here among the friends that hev been kind to me."

"This has come suddenly, Domsie, and is a little upsetting," and Drumsheugh noticed that the Doctor was shaken. "We have worked side by side for a long time, church and school, and I was

THE PASSING OF DOMSIE

hoping that there would be no change till—till we both retired altogether; we're about the same age. Can't you think over it—eh, Dominie?"

"God kens, Doctor, a dinna lik' the thocht o't, but it's for the gude o' the schule. A'm no hearing sae weel as aince a did, an' ma hands are shakin' in the writin'. The scholars are gettin' their due, for a'm no failin' in humanity (Latin), but the ither bairns are losing their share, and ma day's dune.

"Ye 'ill juist say that a'm retirin' an' thank a' body for their consideration, and, Doctor, a've juist a favour tae ask. Gin a new schule an' maister's hoose be built will ye lat me get the auld ane; it 'ill no be worth much an' . . . I wud like tae end ma days there."

"Whate'er you want, Domsie, and ye 'ill come to the Manse till it be free, and we 'ill have many a night among the classics, but . . . this is bad news for the Glen, come who may in your place," and then, though each man did his part bravely, it was a cheerless evening.

Next day Domsie left to make his pious pilgrimage, and on the Sabbath there was only one subject in the kirkyard.

"Div ye no think, neebours," said Hillocks, after a tribute had been paid to Domsie's services, "that he oucht tae get some bit testimonial? It wudna be wiselike tae let him slip oot o' the schule withoot a word frae the Glen."

Hillocks paused, but the fathers were so much

astonished at Hillocks taking the initiative in expenditure that they waited for further speech.

"Noo, Pitscothrie is no a pairish tae pit beside Drumtochty for ae meenut, but when their Dominie gied up his post, if the bodies didna gather fifty pund for him; they ca'd it a purse o' sovereigns in the *Advertiser,* but that was juist a genteel name for't.

"A'm no sayin'," continued Hillocks, "that it wud be safe tae trust Domsie wi' as mickle siller at a time; he wud be off tae Edinburgh an' spend it on auld bukes, or may be divide it up amang his students. He's careless, is Domsie, an' inclined to be wastefu'; but we micht gie him somethin' tae keep."

"What wud ye say," suggested Whinnie, when the kirkyard was revolving the matter, "if we got him a coo 'at wud gie him milk and be a bit troke tae occupy his time? What he didna need cud be made into butter and sent tae Muirtown; it wud be a help."

"Ye have an oreeginal mind," said Jamie, who always on those occasions pitied the woman that was married to Whinnie, "an' a'm sure yir perposal 'll be remembered. Domsie feedin' his coo on the road-side, wi' a Latin buke in his hand, wud be interestin'."

"It's most aggravatin'," broke in Hillocks, who was much annoyed at the turn things had taken, "that ye winna gie me time tae feenish, an' 'ill set

Domsie stravaging the roads at the tail o' a coo for his last days."

"It was Jamie," remonstrated Whinnie.

"Haud yir tongue." Hillocks felt the time was short, and he had an idea that must be ventilated. "A was considerin' that Domsie's snuff-box is gey far thro' wi't. A'm judjin' it has seen thirty years, at ony rate, and it was naethin tae boast o' at the beginnin'. A've seen fresh hinges pit on it twice masel.

"Now, gin we bocht a snod bit silver boxie ain pit an inscription on't wi'

PRESENTED TO

MR. PATRICK JAMIESON,

LATE SCHOOLMASTER OF DRUMTOCHTY,

BY A FEW FRIENDS,

it wud be usefu' for ae thing, it wud be bonnie for anither, aye, an' something mair," and Hillocks grew mysterious.

"A legacy, div ye mean," inquired Jamie, "or what are ye aifter?"

"Weel, ye see," exclaimed Hillocks with much cunning, "there's a man in Kildrummie got a box frae his customers, an' it's never oot o' his hand. When he taps the lid ye can see him reading the inscription, and he's a way o' passin' it tae ye on the slant that's downricht clever. Ye canna help seein' the words."

"Gin we were thinkin' aboot a present tae a

coal agent or a potato dealer," said Jamie, " I wud hae the box wi' the words, but Domsie's a queer body, an' a'm jalousin' that he wud never use yir grand silver box frae the day he got it, an' a'm dootin' it micht be sold fer some laddie to get him better keep at the college.

"Besides," continued Jamie thoughtfully, "a'm no sure that ony man can tak up wi' a new box after fifty. He's got accustomed tae the grip o' the auld box, and he kens whar tae pit in his thumb and finger. A coont that it taks aboot fifteen year tae grow into a snuff-box.

"There's juist ae thing Domsie cares aboot, an' it's naither meat nor drink, nor siller snuff-boxes; it's his college laddies, gettin' them forrit and payin' their fees, an' haudin' them in life till they're dune."

By this time the kirkyard was listening as one man and with both ears, for it was plain Jamie had an idea.

"Ca' on, Jamie," encouraged Drumsheugh, who had as yet given no sign.

"He's hed his ain time, hes Domsie, gaein' roond Muirtown market collectin' the bank notes for his scholars an' seein' they hed their bukes. A'm no denyin' that Domsie was greedy in his ain way, and gin the Glen cud gither eneuch money tae foond a bit bursary for puir scholars o' Drumtochty, a wudna say but that he micht be pleased."

The matter was left in Drumsheugh's hands, with Doctor Davidson as consulting counsel, and he would tell nothing for a fortnight. Then they saw in the Dunleith train that he was charged with tidings, and a meeting was held at the junction, Peter being forbidden to mention time, and commanded to take the outcasts of Kildrummie up by themselves if they couldn't wait.

"The first man a mentioned it tae was oor Saunders, an' he said naethin' at the time, but he cam up in the forenicht, and slippit a note in ma hand. 'He didna pit mickle intae me,' says he, 'but he's daein' fine wi' the bairns.' Neebur, a kent that meenut that the Glen wud dae something handsome.

"Next morning a gied a cry at the Free Manse, and telt Maister Carmichael. If he was na oot o' the room like a man possessed, and he gied me every penny he hed in the hoose, ten pund five shilling. And at the gate he waved his hat in the air, and cries, 'The Jamieson Bursary.'

"It was ae note from one man an' three frae his neebur, an' twa shilling frae the cottars. Abody has dune his pairt, one hundred an' ninety-two pounds frae the Glen.

"We sent a bit letter tae the Drumtochty fouk in the Sooth, and they's sent fifty-eight pounds, wi' mony good wishes, an' what na think ye hev the auld scholars sent? A hundred and forty pounds. An' last nicht we hed three hundred and ninety pounds."

"Ma word!" was all Hillocks found himself able to comment; "that wad get a richt snuff-box."

"Ye hev mair tae tell, Drumsheugh," said Jamie; "feenish the list."

"Yere a wratch, Jamie," responded the treasurer of the Jamieson Bursary Fund. "Hoo did ye ken aboot the Doctor? says he tae me laist nicht, ' here's a letter to Lord Kilspindie. Give it to him at Muirtown, and I would not say but he might make the sum up to four hundred.' So a saw his lordship in his room, and he wrote a cheque and pit in a letter, an' says he, ' Open that in the Bank, Drumsheugh,' an' a did. It was for ten pounds, wi' a hundred on tae't, making up £500. Twenty pund a year tae a Drumtochty scholar for ever. Jamie," said Drumsheugh, "ye've gotten yir bursary."

It was arranged that the meeting of celebration should be held in the parish kirk, which in those days was used for nothing except Divine worship; but the Doctor declared this to be no exception to his rule.

"Kirk and school have been one in Scotland since John Knox's day, and one they shall be while I live in Drumtochty; we 'ill honour him in the kirk, for the good the Dominie has done to the bairns, and to pure learning."

The meeting was delayed till Professor Ross had come home from Australia, with his F.R.S. and all his other honours, for he was marked out to make the presentation; and every Drumtochty scholar within reach was enjoined to attend.

THE PASSING OF DOMSIE

They came from Kildrummie at various hours and in many conveyances, and Hillocks checked the number at the bridge with evident satisfaction.

"Atween yesterday and the day," he reported to Jamie, in the afternoon, "aucht and twenty scholars hae passed, no including the Professor, and there's fower expected by the next train; they'll just be in time," which they were, to everybody's delight.

"It's a gude thing, Hillocks," said Jamie, "that bridge was mended; there's been fifty degrees gane over it the day, Hillocks! to say naithin' o' a wecht o' knowledge."

The Doctor had them all, thirty-three University men, with Domsie and Carmichael and Weelum MacLure, as good a graduate as any man, to dinner, and for that end had his barn wonderfully prepared. Some of the guests have written famous books since then, some are great preachers now, some are chief authorities to science, some have never been heard of beyond a little sphere, some are living, and some are dead; but all have done their part, and each man that night showed, by the grip of his hand, and the look on his face, that he knew where his debt was due.

Domsie sat on the Doctor's right hand, and the Professor on his left, and a great effort was made at easy conversation, Domsie asking the Professor three times whether he had completely recovered from the fever which had frightened them all so much in the Glen, and the Professor congratulating the Doctor at intervals on the decorations of the dinner hall. Domsie pretended to eat, and declared he had never made so hearty a dinner in his life, but his hands could hardly hold the knife and fork, and he was plainly going over the story of each man at the table, while the place rang with reminiscences of the old school among the pines.

Before they left the barn, Doctor Davidson proposed Domsie's health, and the laddies—all laddies that day—drank it, some in wine, some in water, every man from the heart, and then one of them,—they say it was a quiet divine—started, in face of Doctor Davidson, "For he's a jolly good fellow," and there are those who now dare to say that the Doctor joined in with much gusto, but in these days no man's reputation is safe.

Domsie was not able to say much, but he said more than could have been expected. He called them his laddies for the last time, and thanked them for the kindness they were doing their old master. There was not an honour any one of them had won, from a prize in the junior Humanity to the last degree, he could not mention.

Before sitting down he said that they all missed George Howe that day, and that Marget, his mother, had sent her greetings to the scholars.

Then they went to the kirk, where Drumtochty was waiting, and as Domsie came in with his laddies round him the people rose, and would have cheered

THE PASSING OF DOMSIE

had they been elsewhere and some one had led. The Doctor went into the precentor's desk and gave out the hundredth psalm, which is ever sung on great days and can never be sung dry. After which one of the thirty-three thanked the Almighty for all pure knowledge, all good books, all faithful teachers, and besought peace and joy for "our dear master in the evening of his days."

It was the Professor who read the address from the scholars, and this was the last paragraph.

> "Finally, we assure you that none of us can ever forget the parish school of Drumtochty, or fail to hold in tender remembrance the master who first opened to us the way of knowledge, and taught us the love thereof.
> "We are, so long as we live,
> "Your grateful and affectionate
> "SCHOLARS."

Then came the names with all the degrees, and the congregation held their breath to the last M.A.

"Now, Drumsheugh," said the Doctor, and that worthy man made the great speech of his life, expressing the respect of the Glen for Domsie, assigning the glory of a brilliant idea to Jamie Soutar, relating its triumphant accomplishment, describing the Jamieson Bursary, and declaring that while the parish lasted there would be a Jamieson scholar to the honour of Domsie's work. For a while Domsie's voice was very shaky when he was speaking about himself, but afterwards it grew strong and began to vibrate, as he implored the new generation to claim their birthright of learning and to remember that "the poorest parish, though it have but bare fields and humble homes, can yet turn out scholars to be a strength and credit to the commonwealth."

The Professor saw Domsie home, and noticed that he was shaking and did not wish to speak. He said goodbye at the old schoolhouse, and Ross caught him repeating to himself:

> "Eheu fugaces, Postume, Postume,
> Labuntur anni."

but he seemed very content.

Ross rose at daybreak next morning and wandered down to the schoolhouse, recalling at every step his boyhood and early struggles, the goodness of Domsie, and his life of sacrifice. The clearing looked very peaceful, and the sun touched with beauty the old weather-beaten building which had been the nursery of so many scholars, but which would soon be deserted for ever. He pushed the door open and started to see Domsie seated at the well-known desk, and in his right hand firmly clasped the address which the scholars had presented to him. His spectacles were on his forehead, his left elbow was resting on the arm of the chair, and Ross recognised the old look upon his face.

It used to come like a flash when a difficult passage had suddenly yielded up its hidden treasure, and Ross knew that Domsie had seen the Great Secret, and was at last and completely satisfied.

DR. DAVIDSON'S LAST CHRISTMAS

DR. DAVIDSON'S LAST CHRISTMAS

Christmas fell on a Sunday the year Dr. Davidson died, and on the preceding Monday a groom drove up to the Manse from Muirtown Castle.

"A letter, Doctor, from his lordship"—John found his master sitting before the study fire in a reverie, looking old and sad—"and there's a bit boxie in the kitchen."

"Will you see, John, that the messenger has such food as we can offer him?" and the Doctor roused himself at the sight of the familiar handwriting; "there is that, eh, half-fowl that Rebecca was keeping for my dinner to-day; perhaps she could do it up for him. I . . . do not feel hungry to-day. And, John, will you just say that I'm sorry that . . . owing to circumstances, we can't offer him refreshment?" On these occasions the Doctor felt his straitness greatly, having kept a house in his day where man and beast had of the best.

"What dis for the minister of Drumtochty an' his . . . hoose 'ill dae for a groom, even though he serve the Earl o' Kilspindie, an' a' ken better than say onything tae Becca aboot the chuckie;" this he said to himself on his way to the kitchen, where that able woman had put the messenger from the castle in his own place, and was treating him with conspicuous and calculated condescension. He was a man somewhat given to appetite, and critical about his drink, as became a servant of the Earl; but such was the atmosphere of the manse and the awfulness of the Doctor's household that he made a hearty dinner off ham and eggs, with good spring water, and departed declaring his gratitude aloud.

" MY DEAR DAVIDSON,—

"Will you distribute the enclosed trifle among your old pensioners in the Glen as you may see fit, and let it come from you, who would have given them twice as much had it not been for that confounded bank. The port is for yourself, Sandeman's '48—the tipple you and I have tasted together for many a year. If you hand it over to the liquidators, as you wanted to do with the few bottles you had in your cellar, I'll have you up before the Sheriff of Muirtown for breach of trust and embezzlement as sure as my name is

" Your old friend,
"KILSPINDIE."

"P.S.—The Countess joins me in Christmas greetings and charges you to fail us on New Year's Day at your peril. We are anxious about Hay, who has been ordered to the front."

LAST CHRISTMAS

The Doctor opened the cheque and stroked it gently; then he read the letter again and snuffed, using his handkerchief vigorously. After which he wrote:—

"DEAR KILSPINDIE,—

"It is, without exception, the prettiest cheque I have ever had in my hands, and it comes from as good a fellow as ever lived. You knew that it would hurt me not to be able to give my little Christmas gifts, and you have done this kindness. Best thanks from the people and myself, and as for the port, the liquidators will not see a drop of it. Don't believe any of those stories about the economies at the manse which I suspect you have been hearing from Drumtochty. Deliberate falsehoods; we are living like fighting cocks. I'm a little shaky—hint of gout, I fancy—but hope to be with you on New Year's Day. God bless you both, and preserve Hay in the day of battle.

"Yours affectionately,
"ALEXANDER DAVIDSON."

"Don't like that signature, Augusta," said the Earl to his wife; "'yours affectionately' it's true enough, for no man has a warmer heart, but he never wrote that way before. Davidson's breaking up, and . . . he 'ill be missed. I must get Manley to run out here and overhaul him when Davidson comes down on New Year's Day. My belief is that he's been starving himself. Peter Robertson, the land steward, says that he has never touched a drop of wine since that bank smashed; now that won't do at our age, but he's an obstinate fellow, Davidson, when he takes a thing into his head."

The Doctor's determination—after the calamity of the bank failure—to reduce himself to the depths of poverty was wonderful, but Drumtochty was cunning and full of tact. He might surrender his invested means and reserve only one hundred pounds a year out of his living, but when he sent for the Kildrummie auctioneer and instructed him to sell every stick of furniture, except a bare minimum for one sitting-room and a bedroom, Jock accepted the commission at once, and proceeded at eleven miles an hour—having just bought a new horse—to take counsel with Drumsheugh. Next Friday, as a result thereof, he dropped into the factor's office—successor to him over whom the Doctor had triumphed gloriously—and amid an immense variety of rural information, mentioned that he was arranging a sale of household effects at Drumtochty Manse. Jock was never known to be so dilatory with an advertisement before, and ere he got it out Lord Kilspindie had come to terms with the liquidator and settled the Doctor's belongings on him for life.

The Doctor's next effort was with his household, and for weeks the minister looked wistfully at John and Rebecca, till at last he called them in and stated the situation.

"You have both been . . . good and faithful servants to me, indeed I may say . . . friends for many years, and I had hoped you would have remained in the Manse till . . . so long as I was spared. And I may mention now that I had made some slight provision that would have . . . made you comfortable after I was gone."

"It wes kind o' ye, sir, an' mindfu'." Rebecca spoke, not John, and her tone was of one who might have to be firm and must not give herself away by sentiment.

"It is no longer possible for me, through . . . certain events, to live as I have been accustomed to do, and I am afraid that I must . . . do without your help. A woman coming in to cook and . . . such like will be all I can afford."

The expression on the housekeeper's face at this point was such that even the Doctor did not dare to look at her again, but turned to John, whose countenance was inscrutable.

"Your future, John, has been giving me much anxious thought, and I hope to be able to do something with Lord Kilspindie next week. There are many quiet places on the estate which might suit . . ." then the Doctor weakened, "although I know well no place will ever be like Drumtochty, and the old Manse will never be the same . . .

without you. But you see how it is . . . friends."

"Doctor Davidson," and he knew it was vain to escape her, "wi' yir permission a' wud like tae ask ye ane or twa questions, an' ye 'ill forgie the leeberty. Dis ony man in the Pairish o' Drumtochty ken yir wys like John? Wha 'ill tak yir messages, an' prepare the fouk for the veesitation, an' keep the gairden snod, an' see tae a' yir trokes when John's awa? Wull ony man ever cairry the bukes afore ye like John?"

"Never," admitted the Doctor, "never."

"Div ye expect the new wumman 'ill ken hoo mickle stairch tae pit in yir stock, an' hoo mickle butter ye like on yir chicken, an' when ye change yir flannels tae a day, an' when ye like anither blanket on yir bed, an' the wy tae mak the currant drink for yir cold?"

"No, no, Rebecca, nobody will ever be so good to me as you've been"—the Doctor was getting very shaky.

"Then what for wud ye send us awa, and bring in some handless, useless tawpie that cud neither cook ye a decent meal nor keep the Manse wise like? Is't for room? The Manse is as big as ever. Is't for meat? We 'ill eat less than she 'ill waste."

"You know better, Rebecca," said the Doctor, attempting to clear his throat; "it's because . . . because I cannot afford to . . ."

"A' ken very weel, an' John an' me hev settled

that. For thirty year ye've paid us better than ony minister's man an' manse hoosekeeper in Perthshire, an' ye wantit tae raise oor wages aifter we mairrit. Div ye ken what John an' me hev in the bank for oor laist days?"

The Doctor only shook his head, being cowed for once in his life.

"Atween us, five hundred and twenty-sax pund."

"Eleven an' sevenpence," added John, steadying his voice with arithmetic.

"It's five year sin we askit ye tae py naethin' mair, but juist gie's oor keep, an' noo the time's come, an' welcome. Hev John or me ever disobeyed ye or spoken back a' thae years?"

The Doctor only made a sign with his hand.

"We 'ill dae't aince, at ony rate, for ye may gie us notice tae leave an' order us oot o' the manse; but here we stop till we're no fit tae serve ye or ye hae nae mair need o' oor service."

"A homologate that"—it was a brave word, and one of which John was justly proud, but he did not quite make the most of it that day.

"I thank you from my heart, and . . . I'll never speak of parting again," and for the first time they saw tears on the Doctor's cheek.

"John," Rebecca turned on her husband—no man would have believed it of the beadle of Drumtochty, but he was also . . . "what are ye stoiterin' roond the table for? it's time tae set the Doctor's denner; as for that chicken——" and Rebecca retired to the kitchen, having touched her highest point that day.

The insurrection in the manse oozed out, and encouraged a conspiracy of rebellion in which even the meekest people were concerned. Jean Baxter, of Burnbrae, who had grasped greedily at the dairy contract of the manse, when the glebe was let to Netherton, declined to render any account to Rebecca, and the Doctor had to take the matter in hand.

"There's a little business, Mrs. Baxter, I would like to settle with you, as I happen to be here." The Doctor had dropped in on his way back from Whinny Knowe, where Marget and he had been talking of George for two hours. "You know that I have to be, eh . . . careful now and I . . . you will let me pay what we owe for that delicious butter you are good enough to supply."

"Ye 'ill surely tak a look roond the fields first, Doctor, an' tell's what ye think o' the crops;" and after that it was necessary for him to take tea. Again and again he was foiled, but he took a firm stand by the hydrangea in the garden, where he had given them Lord Kilspindie's message, and John Baxter stood aside that the affair might be decided in single combat.

"Now, Mrs. Baxter, before leaving, I must insist," began the Doctor with authority, and his stick was in his hand; but Jean saw a geographical advantage, and seized it instantly.

"Div ye mind, sir, comin' tae this gairden five year syne this month, and stannin' on that verra spot aside the hydrangy?"

The Doctor scented danger, but he could not retreat.

"Weel, at ony rate, John an' me dinna forget that day, an' never wull, for we were makin' ready tae leave the home o' the Baxters for mony generations wi' a heavy heart, an' it wes you that stoppit us. Ye 'ill maybe no mind what ye said tae me."

"We 'ill not talk of that to-day, Mrs. Baxter . . . that's past and over."

"Aye, it's past, but it's no over, Doctor Davidson; na, na, John an' me wesna made that wy. Ye may lauch at a fulish auld wife, but ilka kirnin' (churning) day ye veesit us again. When a'm turnin' the kirn a' see ye comin' up the road as ye did that day, an' a' gar the handle keep time wi' yir step; when a' tak oot the bonnie yellow butter ye're stannin' in the gairden, an' then a' stamp ae pund wi' buttercups, an' a' say, 'You're not away yet, Burnbrae, you're not away yet'— that wes yir word tae the gude man; and when the ither stamp comes doon on the second pund and leaves the bonnie daisies on't, 'Better late than never, Burnbrae; better late than never, Burnbrae.' Ye said that afore ye left, Doctor."

Baxter was amazed at his wife, and the Doctor saw himself defeated.

"Mony a time hes John an' me sat in the summer-hoose an' brocht back that day, an' mony a time hev we wantit tae dae somethin' for him that keepit the auld roof-tree abune oor heads. God forgie me, Doctor, but when a' heard ye hed gien up yir glebe ma hert loupit, an' a' said tae John, 'The'ill no want for butter at the manse sae lang as there's a Baxter in Burnbrae.'

"Dinna be angry, sir," but the flush that brought the Doctor's face unto a state of perfection was not anger. "A' ken it's a leeberty we're takin', an' maybe a'm presumin' ower far, but gin ye kent hoo sair oor herts were wi' gratitude ye wudna deny us this kindness."

"Ye 'ill lat the Doctor come awa noo, gude wife, tae see the young horse," and Doctor Davidson was grateful to Burnbrae for covering his retreat.

This spirit spread till Hillocks lifted up his horn, outwitting the Doctor with his attentions, and reducing him to submission. When the beadle dropped in upon Hillocks one day, and, after a hasty review of harvest affairs, mentioned that Doctor Davidson was determined to walk in future to and from Kildrummie Station, the worthy man rose without a word, and led the visitor to the shed where his marvellous dog-cart was kept.

"Div ye think that a' cud daur?" studying his general appearance with diffidence.

"There's nae sayin' hoo it micht look wi' a wash," suggested John.

"Sall, it's fell snod noo," after two hours' honest

labour, in which John condescended to share, "an' the gude wife 'ill cover the cushions. Dinna lat on, but a'll be at the gate the morn afore the Doctor starts," and Peter Bruce gave it to be understood that when Hillocks convoyed the Doctor to the compartment of the third rigidly and unanimously reserved for him, his manner, both of walk and conversation was changed, and it is certain that a visit he made to Piggie Walker on the return journey was unnecessary save for the purpose of vain boasting. It was not, however, to be heard of by the Doctor that Hillocks should leave his work at intervals to drive him to Kildrummie, and so there was a war of tactics, in which the one endeavoured to escape past the bridge without detection, while the other swooped down upon him with the dog-cart. On the Wednesday when the Doctor went to Muirtown to buy his last gifts to Drumtochty, he was very cunning, and ran the blockade while Hillocks was in the corn room, but the dog-cart was waiting for him in the evening—Hillocks having been called to Kildrummie by unexpected business, at least so he said—and it was a great satisfaction afterwards to Peter Bruce that he placed fourteen parcels below the seat and fastened eight behind—besides three which the Doctor held in his hands, being fragile, and two, soft goods, on which Hillocks sat for security. For there were twenty-seven humble friends whom the Doctor wished to bless on Christmas Day.

When he bade the minister good-bye at his gate, Hillocks prophesied a storm, and it was of such a kind that on Sunday morning the snow was knee deep on the path from the manse to the kirk, and had drifted up four feet against the door through which the Doctor was accustomed to enter in procession.

"This is unfortunate, very unfortunate," when John reported the state of affairs to the Doctor, "and we must just do the best we can in the circumstances, eh?"

"What wud be yir wull, sir?" but John's tone did not encourage any concessions.

"Well, it would never do for you to be going down bare-headed on such a day, and it's plain we can't get in at the front door. What do you say to taking in the books by the side door, and I'll just come down in my top coat, when the people are gathered"; but the Doctor did not show a firm mind, and it was evident that he was thinking less of himself than of John.

"A'll come for ye at the usual 'oor," was all that functionary deigned to reply, and at a quarter to twelve he brought the gown and bands to the study —he himself being in full black.

"The drift 'ill no tribble ye, an' ye 'ill no need tae gang roond; na, na," and John could not quite conceal his satisfaction, "we 'ill no start on the side door aifter five and thirty years o' the front."

So the two old men—John bare-headed, the Doctor in full canonicals and wearing his college cap—came down on a fair pathway between two banks of snow three feet high, which Saunders from Drumsheugh and a dozen plowmen had piled on either side. The kirk had a severe look that day, with hardly any women or children to relieve the blackness of the men, and the drifts reaching to the sills of the windows, while a fringe of snow draped their sides.

The Doctor's subject was the love of God, and it was noticed that he did not read, but spoke as if he had been in his study. He also dwelt so affectingly on the gift of Christ, and made so tender an appeal unto his people, that Drumsheugh blew his nose with vigour, and Hillocks himself was shaken. After they had sung the paraphrase—

"To Him that lov'd the souls of men,
And washed us in His blood,"

the Doctor charged those present to carry his greetings to the folk at home, and tell them they were all in his heart. After which he looked at his people as they stood for at least a minute, and then lifting his hands, according to the ancient fashion of the Scottish Kirk, he blessed them. His gifts, with a special message to each person, he sent by faithful messengers, and afterwards he went out through the snow to make two visits. The first was to blind Marjorie, who was Free Kirk, but to whom he had shown much kindness all her life. His talk with her was usually of past days and country affairs, seasoned with wholesome humour to cheer her heart, but to-day he fell into another vein, to her great delight, and they spoke of the dispensations of Providence.

"'Whom the Lord loveth, he chasteneth,' Marjorie, is a very instructive Scripture, and I was thinking of it last night. You have had a long and hard trial, but you have doubtless been blessed, for if you have not seen outward things, you have seen the things . . . of the soul." The Doctor hesitated once or twice, as one who had not long travelled this road.

"You and I are about the same age, Marjorie, and we must soon . . . depart. My life was very . . . prosperous, but lately it has pleased the Almighty to . . . chasten me. I have now, therefore, some hope also that I may be one of His children."

"He wes aye gude grain, the Doctor," Marjorie said to her friend after he had left, "but he's hed a touch o' the harvest sun, and he's been ripening."

Meanwhile the Doctor had gone on to Tochty Lodge, and was standing in the stone hall, which was stripped and empty of the Carnegies for ever. Since he was a laddie in a much-worn kilt and a glengarry bonnet without tails, he had gone in and out the Lodge, and himself had seen four generations—faintly remembering the General's grandfather. Every inch of the house was familiar to him, and associated with kindly incidents. He identified the spaces on the walls where the por-

traits of the cavaliers and their ladies had hung;
he went up to the room where the lairds had died
and his friend had hoped to fall on sleep; he visited
the desolate gallery where Kate had held court and
seemed to begin a better day for the old race; then
he returned and stood before the fireplace in which
he had sat long ago and looked up to see the stars in
the sky. Round that hearth many a company of
brave men and fair women had gathered, and now
there remained of this ancient stock but two exiles—
one eating out his heart in poverty and city life,
and a girl who had for weal or woe, God only knew,
passed out of the line of her traditions. A heap of
snow had gathered on the stone, where the honest
wood fire had once burned cheerily, and a gust of
wind coming down the vast open chimney powdered
his coat with drift. It was to him a sign that the
past was closed, and that he would never again
stand beneath that roof.

He opened the gate of the manse, and then,
under a sudden impulse, went on through deep
snow to the village and made a third visit—to
Archie Moncur, whom he found sitting before the
fire reading the *Temperance Trumpet*. Was there
ever a man like Archie?—so gentle and fierce, so
timid and fearless, so modest and persevering. He
would stoop to lift a vagrant caterpillar from the
cart track, and yet had not adjectives to describe
the infamy of a publican; he would hardly give
an opinion on the weather, but he fought the drink-

ing customs of the Glen like a lion; he would only sit in the lowest seat in any place, but every winter he organised—at great trouble and cost of his slender means—temperance meetings which were the fond jest of the Glen. From year to year he toiled on, without encouragement, without success, hopeful, uncomplaining, resolute, unselfish, with the soul of a saint and the spirit of a hero in his poor, deformed, suffering little body. He humbled himself before the very bairns, and allowed an abject like Milton to browbeat him with Pharisaism, but every man in the Glen knew that Archie would have gone to the stake for the smallest jot or tittle of his faith.

"Archie," said the Doctor, who would not sit down, and whose coming had thrown the good man into speechless confusion, "it's the day of our Lord's birth, and I wish to give you and all my friends of the Free Kirk—as you have no minister just now—hearty Christmas greeting. May peace be in your kirk and homes . . . and hearts.

"My thoughts have been travelling back of late over those years since I was ordained minister of this parish and the things which have happened, and it seemed to me that no man has done his duty by his neighbour or before God with a more single heart than you, Archie.

"God bless you." Then on the doorstep the Doctor shook hands again and paused for a minute.

" You have fought a good fight, Archie—I wish we could all say the same . . . a good fight."

For an hour Archie was so dazed that he was not able to say a word, and could do nothing but look into the fire, and then he turned to his sisters, with that curious little movement of the hand which seemed to assist his speech.

"The language wes clean redeeklus, but it wes kindly meant . . . an' it maks up for mony things. . . . The Doctor wes aye a gentleman, an' noo . . . ye can see that he's . . . something mair."

Drumsheugh dined with the Doctor that night, and after dinner John opened for them a bottle of Lord Kilspindie's wine.

"It is the only drink we have in the house, for I have not been using anything of that kind lately, and I think we may have a glass together for the sake of Auld Lang Syne."

They had three toasts, "The Queen," and "The Kirk of Scotland," and "The friends that are far awa," after which—for the last included both the living and the dead—they sat in silence. Then the Doctor began to speak of his ministry, lamenting that he had not done better for his people, and declaring that if he were spared he intended to preach more frequently about the Lord Jesus Christ.

"You and I, Drumsheugh, will have to go a long journey soon, and give an account of our lives in Drumtochty. Perhaps we have done our best as men can, and I think we have tried; but there are many things we might have done otherwise, and some we ought not to have done at all.

"It seems to me now, the less we say in that day of the past the better. . . . We shall wish for mercy rather than justice, and"—here the Doctor looked earnestly over his glasses at his elder—"we would be none the worse, Drumsheugh, of a friend to . . . say a good word for us both in the great court."

"A've thocht that masel"—it was an agony for Drumsheugh to speak—"mair than aince. Weelum MacLure wes . . . ettlin' (feeling) aifter the same thing the nicht he slippit awa, an' gin ony man cud hae studo on his ain feet . . . yonder, it was . . . Weelum."

The Doctor read the last chapter of the Revelation of St. John at prayers that evening with much solemnity, and thereafter prayed concerning those who had lived together in the Glen that they might meet at last in the City.

"Finally, most merciful Father, we thank Thee for Thy patience with us and the goodness Thou hast bestowed upon us, and for as much as Thy servants have sinned against Thee beyond our knowledge, we beseech Thee to judge us not according to our deserts, but according to the merits and intercession of Jesus Christ our Lord." He also pronounced the benediction—which was not his wont at family worship—and he shook hands with his two retainers; but he went with his guest to the outer door.

"Good-bye, Drumsheugh . . . you have been . . . a faithful friend and elder."

When John paid his usual visit to the study before he went to bed, the Doctor did not hear him enter the room. He was holding converse with Skye, who was seated on a chair, looking very wise and much interested.

"Ye're a bonnie beastie, Skye"—like all Scots, the Doctor in his tender moments dropped into dialect—"for a'thing He made is verra gude. Ye've been true and kind to your master, Skye, and ye 'ill miss him if he leaves ye. Some day ye 'ill die also, and they 'ill bury ye, and I doubt that 'ill be the end o' ye, Skye.

"Ye never heard o' God, Skye, or the Saviour, for ye're juist a puir doggie; but your master is minister of Drumtochty, and . . . a sinner saved . . . by grace."

The Doctor was so much affected as he said the last words slowly to himself that John went out on tiptoe, and twice during the night listened—fancying he heard Skye whine. In the morning the Doctor was still sitting in his big chair, and Skye was fondly licking a hand that would never again caress him, while a miniature of Daisy—the little maid who had died in her teens, and whom her brother had loved to his old age—lay on the table, and the Bible was again open at the description of the New Jerusalem.

www.ingramcontent.com/pod-product-compliance
Lightning Source LLC
Chambersburg PA
CBHW021337300426
44114CB00012B/987